# First World War
and Army of Occupation
# War Diary
France, Belgium and Germany

3 DIVISION
Divisional Troops
Divisional Ammunition Column
and Trench Mortar Batteries
5 August 1914 - 31 December 1917

WO95/1402

The Naval & Military Press Ltd
www.nmarchive.com
Published in association with The National Archives

Published by

## The Naval & Military Press Ltd

Unit 10 Ridgewood Industrial Park,

Uckfield, East Sussex,

TN22 5QE England

Tel: +44 (0) 1825 749494

www.naval-military-press.com

www.nmarchive.com

*This diary has been reprinted in facsimile from the original. Any imperfections are inevitably reproduced and the quality may fall short of modern type and cartographic standards.*

© **Crown Copyright**
**Images reproduced by permission of The National Archives, London, England, 2015.**

# Contents

| Document type | Place/Title | Date From | Date To |
|---|---|---|---|
| Heading | Division Ammunition Column. 1914 Aug To 1919 Sept Trench Mortar Bty's 1915 July To 1919 Feb | | |
| Heading | 3rd Divl Ammunition Column Aug-Dec 1914 | | |
| Heading | 3rd Divisional Artillery. Copy of War Diary. 3rd Divisional Ammunition Column R.F.A. August 1914 | | |
| Heading | 3rd Divl. Ammunition Column Vol I 5 VIII 1914-30 VIII 1914 | | |
| War Diary | Hilsea | 05/08/1914 | 06/08/1914 |
| War Diary | Bulford | 07/08/1914 | 18/08/1914 |
| War Diary | Southampton | 19/08/1914 | 19/08/1914 |
| War Diary | Boulogne | 20/08/1914 | 21/08/1914 |
| War Diary | Valencienes Sultain Bavai | 22/08/1914 | 22/08/1914 |
| War Diary | Belgium Reiz De Erzelle | 23/08/1914 | 23/08/1914 |
| War Diary | Mons | 23/08/1914 | 23/08/1914 |
| War Diary | Battle Of Mons | 23/08/1914 | 23/08/1914 |
| War Diary | Hon | 24/08/1914 | 24/08/1914 |
| War Diary | S Waast | 24/08/1914 | 24/08/1914 |
| War Diary | Bavai | 24/08/1914 | 24/08/1914 |
| War Diary | Battle Of Mons | 24/08/1914 | 24/08/1914 |
| War Diary | Amfroipret | 24/08/1914 | 25/08/1914 |
| War Diary | Louvignies Salesches Solesmes Troisville Bertry | 25/08/1914 | 25/08/1914 |
| War Diary | Battle Of Le Cateau | 26/08/1914 | 26/08/1914 |
| War Diary | Serain | 26/08/1914 | 26/08/1914 |
| War Diary | Nr Serain | 26/08/1914 | 26/08/1914 |
| War Diary | St. Quentin. Ham. | 27/08/1914 | 27/08/1914 |
| War Diary | S Quentin Ham. | 26/08/1914 | 27/08/1914 |
| War Diary | Le Cateau Beaurevoir | 26/08/1914 | 26/08/1914 |
| War Diary | Gricourt St Quentin | 27/08/1914 | 27/08/1914 |
| War Diary | Ham | 27/08/1914 | 27/08/1914 |
| War Diary | Le Cateau | 26/08/1914 | 27/08/1914 |
| War Diary | Noyon Carle Pont Pontoise | 28/08/1914 | 28/08/1914 |
| War Diary | Pontoise Bailly | 29/08/1914 | 29/08/1914 |
| War Diary | S Leger | 29/08/1914 | 29/08/1914 |
| War Diary | Choisy Au Bac | 30/08/1914 | 30/08/1914 |
| War Diary | Montigny | 30/08/1914 | 30/08/1914 |
| Heading | 3rd Divisional Artillery. Original War Diary. 3rd Divisional Ammunition Column R F A August 1914 | | |
| War Diary | Hilsea | 05/08/1914 | 06/08/1914 |
| War Diary | Bulford | 07/08/1914 | 20/08/1914 |
| War Diary | Boulogne | 21/08/1914 | 21/08/1914 |
| War Diary | Valenciennes | 22/08/1914 | 22/08/1914 |
| War Diary | Bavai Noirchain Hon | 23/08/1914 | 23/08/1914 |
| War Diary | St Waast Amphroipret Bavai | 24/08/1914 | 24/08/1914 |
| War Diary | Vendegies Troisvilles Bertry | 25/08/1914 | 25/08/1914 |
| War Diary | Elincourt | 26/08/1914 | 26/08/1914 |
| War Diary | Malincourt Elincourt | 26/08/1914 | 26/08/1914 |
| War Diary | Clary | 26/08/1914 | 26/08/1914 |
| War Diary | Maretz | 26/08/1914 | 26/08/1914 |
| War Diary | Seram | 26/08/1914 | 26/08/1914 |
| War Diary | Estrees | 26/08/1914 | 26/08/1914 |

| | | | |
|---|---|---|---|
| War Diary | St Quentin | 27/08/1914 | 27/08/1914 |
| War Diary | Ham | 27/08/1914 | 27/08/1914 |
| War Diary | Noyon | 27/08/1914 | 27/08/1914 |
| War Diary | Sempigny | 27/08/1914 | 27/08/1914 |
| War Diary | Choisis Au Bac | 28/08/1914 | 29/08/1914 |
| War Diary | Montigny | 30/08/1914 | 30/08/1914 |
| War Diary | Levignen | 31/08/1914 | 31/08/1914 |
| Heading | 3rd Divisional Artillery. 3rd Divisional Ammunition Column R.F.A. September 1914 | | |
| War Diary | Bouillancy | 01/09/1914 | 01/09/1914 |
| War Diary | Bregy | 01/09/1914 | 01/09/1914 |
| War Diary | Montigny | 02/09/1914 | 02/09/1914 |
| War Diary | Trilbardou | 02/09/1914 | 02/09/1914 |
| War Diary | Crecy | 02/09/1914 | 02/09/1914 |
| War Diary | La Haute Maison | 02/09/1914 | 02/09/1914 |
| War Diary | Grande Loge Fme | 03/09/1914 | 03/09/1914 |
| War Diary | La Barde | 03/09/1914 | 03/09/1914 |
| War Diary | Paris | 04/09/1914 | 04/09/1914 |
| War Diary | Guerard | 04/09/1914 | 04/09/1914 |
| War Diary | Montcerf | 04/09/1914 | 04/09/1914 |
| War Diary | La Houssaye | 04/09/1914 | 04/09/1914 |
| War Diary | Chateau Des Boulayes | 04/09/1914 | 04/09/1914 |
| War Diary | Chatres | 05/09/1914 | 05/09/1914 |
| War Diary | Liverdy | 05/09/1914 | 05/09/1914 |
| War Diary | Retal | 05/09/1914 | 05/09/1914 |
| War Diary | Villepayen | 05/09/1914 | 05/09/1914 |
| War Diary | Champrose | 06/09/1914 | 06/09/1914 |
| War Diary | Livardy | 07/09/1914 | 07/09/1914 |
| War Diary | Lumigny | 07/09/1914 | 07/09/1914 |
| War Diary | Coullomlers | 08/09/1914 | 08/09/1914 |
| War Diary | St Pierre En Veuve | 08/09/1914 | 08/09/1914 |
| War Diary | Les Brosse | 08/09/1914 | 08/09/1914 |
| War Diary | Rebais | 09/09/1914 | 09/09/1914 |
| War Diary | Nanteuil | 10/09/1914 | 10/09/1914 |
| War Diary | Veuilly | 11/09/1914 | 11/09/1914 |
| War Diary | Montreuil | 11/09/1914 | 11/09/1914 |
| War Diary | Mery | 11/09/1914 | 11/09/1914 |
| War Diary | Dammard | 11/09/1914 | 11/09/1914 |
| War Diary | Neuvilly | 12/09/1914 | 12/09/1914 |
| War Diary | Oulchy La Ville | 12/09/1914 | 12/09/1914 |
| War Diary | Grand Rozoy | 12/09/1914 | 12/09/1914 |
| War Diary | Braine | 13/09/1914 | 29/09/1914 |
| War Diary | Lesges | 30/09/1914 | 30/09/1914 |
| Heading | 3rd Divisional Artillery. 3rd Divisional Ammunition Column R.F.A. October 1914 | | |
| War Diary | Chouy | 01/10/1914 | 03/10/1914 |
| War Diary | La Ferte Milon | 04/10/1914 | 04/10/1914 |
| War Diary | Crepy | 05/10/1914 | 05/10/1914 |
| War Diary | Crepy En Valoise | 06/10/1914 | 06/10/1914 |
| War Diary | Verberie | 07/10/1914 | 07/10/1914 |
| War Diary | Verberie Pontremy | 08/10/1914 | 08/10/1914 |
| War Diary | Le Plessiel | 09/10/1914 | 09/10/1914 |
| War Diary | Le Plessiel Incourt | 10/10/1914 | 10/10/1914 |
| War Diary | Sains | 11/10/1914 | 11/10/1914 |
| War Diary | Auchel Allouagne | 12/10/1914 | 12/10/1914 |
| War Diary | Locon | 13/10/1914 | 28/10/1914 |

| | | | |
|---|---|---|---|
| War Diary | L'Epinette | 29/10/1914 | 30/10/1914 |
| War Diary | Lestrem | 31/10/1914 | 31/10/1914 |
| Heading | 3rd Divisional Ammunition Column 3rd Divisional Ammunition Column R.F.A. November 1914 | | |
| War Diary | Lestrem | 01/11/1914 | 13/11/1914 |
| War Diary | Ferme Du Prince | 14/11/1914 | 14/11/1914 |
| War Diary | Vieux Berquin | 15/11/1914 | 18/11/1914 |
| War Diary | Reninghelst | 19/11/1914 | 19/11/1914 |
| War Diary | Berthen | 20/11/1914 | 30/11/1914 |
| Heading | 3rd Divisional Artillery. 3rd Divisional Ammunition Column R.F.A. December 1914 | | |
| War Diary | Berthen | 01/12/1914 | 01/12/1914 |
| War Diary | Near Mont Noir | 14/12/1914 | 16/12/1914 |
| War Diary | Berthen | 17/12/1914 | 29/12/1914 |
| War Diary | St Jans Cappel | 30/12/1914 | 31/12/1914 |
| Heading | R.F.A. Ammunition Column War Diary, Jan-Dec., 1915 | | |
| War Diary | In Gans Cappels | 01/01/1915 | 31/01/1915 |
| Heading | 121/4516 3rd Divl Ammun Coln Vol II 1st Feb To 31st March 1915 | | |
| War Diary | St. Jans Cappel | 01/02/1915 | 31/03/1915 |
| Heading | 121/5255 3rd Divl Ammun Coln Vol III 1-30.4.15 | | |
| War Diary | St Jans Cappel (France) | 01/04/1915 | 08/04/1915 |
| War Diary | Ouderdom (Belgium) | 01/04/1915 | 01/04/1915 |
| War Diary | Westoutre Boescheppe | 09/04/1915 | 09/04/1915 |
| War Diary | Westoutre Boescheppe Reninghelst | 10/04/1915 | 30/04/1915 |
| War Diary | A Form. Messages And Signals. | | |
| Miscellaneous | A Form. Messages And Signals. | | |
| Heading | 121/5444 3rd Divl Ammun Coln Vol IV 1-31.5.15 | | |
| War Diary | H. Qrs No. 1 Sec | | |
| War Diary | Westoutre (B) No. 2. Sec | | |
| War Diary | Boeschepe (F) No. 3 Sec | | |
| War Diary | Reninghelst (B) No. 4 Sec | | |
| War Diary | | 30/05/1915 | 31/05/1915 |
| War Diary | Poperinghe (B) | 31/05/1915 | 31/05/1915 |
| War Diary | Busseboom (B) | 31/05/1915 | 31/05/1915 |
| War Diary | | 24/05/1915 | 31/05/1915 |
| War Diary | | 02/05/1915 | 31/05/1915 |
| War Diary | | 27/05/1915 | 27/05/1915 |
| Heading | 121/5842 3rd Division 3rd Divl. Ammun Coln Vol V 1-30.6.15 | | |
| War Diary | | 01/06/1915 | 01/06/1915 |
| War Diary | Belgium | 01/06/1915 | 04/06/1915 |
| War Diary | Poperinghe | 05/06/1915 | 18/06/1915 |
| War Diary | Hooge | 17/06/1915 | 19/06/1915 |
| War Diary | Poperinghe | 19/06/1915 | 30/06/1915 |
| War Diary | | 12/06/1915 | 12/06/1915 |
| War Diary | | 04/06/1915 | 25/06/1915 |
| Heading | 121/6242 3rd Division 3rd Divl Ammun Coln Vol VI 1-30.7.15 (7) | | |
| War Diary | In Bivouac Poperinghe | 01/07/1915 | 07/07/1915 |
| War Diary | Abeele | 07/07/1915 | 07/07/1915 |
| War Diary | Poperinghe | 07/07/1915 | 25/07/1915 |
| War Diary | Abeele | 08/07/1915 | 30/07/1915 |
| War Diary | | 04/07/1915 | 12/07/1915 |

| | | | |
|---|---|---|---|
| Heading | 121/6567 3rd Division 3rd Divl Ammun Coln Vol VII From 1-31.8.15 | | |
| War Diary | | 01/08/1915 | 29/08/1915 |
| War Diary | | 01/08/1915 | 31/08/1915 |
| Heading | 121/6918 3rd Division 3rd Divl Ammun Coln Vol VIII 1-30 Sept 15 | | |
| War Diary | | 01/09/1915 | 26/09/1915 |
| War Diary | | 08/09/1915 | 20/09/1915 |
| Heading | 121/7368 3rd ivision 3rd Divl Ammun Coln Vol IX Oct 15 | | |
| War Diary | In Billets 1 Miles W Of Poperinghe | 01/10/1915 | 26/10/1915 |
| War Diary | | 19/10/1915 | 23/10/1915 |
| Heading | 121/7655 3rd Division 3rd Divl Ammn Col. Nov Vol X | | |
| War Diary | | 01/11/1915 | 25/11/1915 |
| War Diary | | 11/11/1915 | 23/11/1915 |
| Heading | 121/7957 3rd Divl Ammn Col. Dec Vol XI | | |
| War Diary | | 01/12/1915 | 30/12/1915 |
| Heading | 3rd Division Divl. Artillery 3rd Divisional Ammn Col. Jan-Dec 1916 | | |
| Heading | 3rd Divisional Artillery. 3rd Divisional Ammunition Column January 1916 | | |
| War Diary | | 01/01/1916 | 13/01/1916 |
| Heading | 3rd Divisional Artillery. 3rd Divisional Ammunition Column February 1916 | | |
| War Diary | | 01/02/1916 | 29/02/1916 |
| War Diary | Zouafques | 04/02/1916 | 29/02/1916 |
| Heading | 3rd Divisional Artillery. 3rd Divisional Ammunition Column March 1916 | | |
| War Diary | Zouafques | 01/03/1916 | 11/03/1916 |
| War Diary | Bueschepe | 26/03/1916 | 26/03/1916 |
| War Diary | | 16/03/1916 | 22/03/1916 |
| Heading | 3rd Divisional Artillery. 3rd Divisional Ammunition Column April 1916 | | |
| War Diary | Boeschepe | 01/04/1916 | 12/04/1916 |
| Heading | 3rd Divisional Artillery. 3rd Divisional Ammunition Column May 1916 | | |
| War Diary | Godewaersvelde | 01/05/1916 | 01/05/1916 |
| War Diary | Berthen | 09/05/1916 | 16/05/1916 |
| War Diary | Postmip Away | 09/05/1916 | 23/05/1916 |
| War Diary | | 12/05/1916 | 12/05/1916 |
| War Diary | | 01/05/1916 | 01/05/1916 |
| War Diary | Postmgsh D A C | 20/05/1916 | 25/05/1916 |
| Heading | 3rd Divisional Artillery. 3rd Divisional Ammunition Column June 1916 | | |
| War Diary | Godewaersvelde | 01/06/1916 | 18/06/1916 |
| War Diary | Postingsche | 01/06/1918 | 01/06/1918 |
| War Diary | Poshed La D A C | 18/06/1918 | 29/06/1918 |
| Heading | 3rd Divisional Artillery. 3rd Divl. Ammunition Column. July 1916 | | |
| War Diary | Seninghem | 01/07/1916 | 18/07/1916 |
| Heading | 3rd Divisional Artillery 3rd Divisional Ammunition Column August 1916 | | |
| War Diary | | 01/08/1916 | 15/08/1916 |
| Heading | 3rd Divisional Artillery. 3rd Divl. Ammunition Column. September 1916 | | |
| War Diary | | 01/09/1916 | 27/09/1916 |

| | | | |
|---|---|---|---|
| Heading | 3rd Divisional Artillery. 3rd Divl. Ammunition Column. October 1916 | | |
| War Diary | Still At Chatean La Tourniere | 01/10/1916 | 17/10/1916 |
| Heading | 3rd Divisional Artillery. 3rd Divl. Ammunition Column. November 1916 | | |
| War Diary | | 01/11/1916 | 20/11/1916 |
| Heading | 3rd Divisional Artillery. 3rd Divl. Ammunition Column. December 1916 | | |
| War Diary | | 01/12/1916 | 16/12/1916 |
| Heading | 3rd Division War Diary D.A.C. January To December 1917 | | |
| War Diary | | 01/01/1917 | 29/05/1917 |
| War Diary | Arras | 01/06/1917 | 01/06/1917 |
| War Diary | Tilloy | 22/06/1917 | 22/06/1917 |
| War Diary | Achicourt | 22/06/1917 | 23/06/1917 |
| War Diary | Arras | 24/06/1917 | 24/06/1917 |
| War Diary | Simencourt | 01/07/1917 | 01/07/1917 |
| War Diary | Bapaume | 07/07/1917 | 21/08/1917 |
| War Diary | | 21/08/1917 | 21/08/1917 |
| War Diary | Mill Cross | 01/09/1917 | 29/09/1917 |
| War Diary | G 10 B Sheet 28 | 01/10/1917 | 27/10/1917 |
| War Diary | Bapaume | 30/11/1917 | 30/11/1917 |
| War Diary | | 12/12/1917 | 24/12/1917 |
| Heading | 3rd Divisional Divl. Artillery 3rd Divl. Ammn Column 1918 | | |
| War Diary | Gomie Court | 31/01/1918 | 01/02/1918 |
| War Diary | Henu | 11/02/1918 | 28/02/1918 |
| Heading | 3rd Divisional Artillery. 3rd Divisional Ammunition Column R.F.A. March 1918 | | |
| War Diary | Henu | 01/03/1918 | 01/03/1918 |
| War Diary | Gaudiempre | 01/03/1918 | 01/03/1918 |
| War Diary | Liendecourt | 02/03/1918 | 23/03/1918 |
| War Diary | Bretencourt | 24/03/1918 | 30/03/1918 |
| War Diary | Bavincourt | 30/03/1918 | 31/03/1918 |
| Miscellaneous | 3rd Divisional Artillery War Diary 3rd Divisional Ammunition Column April 1918 | | |
| War Diary | Bavincourt | 01/04/1918 | 15/04/1918 |
| War Diary | Lapugnoy | 01/05/1918 | 16/05/1918 |
| War Diary | | 13/05/1918 | 16/05/1918 |
| War Diary | | 01/06/1918 | 29/06/1918 |
| War Diary | D 8d 2.3 (Bethune Combined Sheet) | 01/07/1918 | 01/07/1918 |
| War Diary | D 8d 2.3 | 01/08/1918 | 01/08/1918 |
| War Diary | B 8c 4.7 | 07/08/1918 | 07/08/1918 |
| War Diary | Nedon | 13/08/1918 | 13/08/1918 |
| War Diary | Canettemont | 14/08/1918 | 14/08/1918 |
| War Diary | Humbercamp | 20/08/1918 | 23/08/1918 |
| War Diary | Pommier | 25/08/1918 | 25/08/1918 |
| War Diary | Adinper Wood | 28/08/1918 | 01/09/1918 |
| War Diary | Boiry St Rictrude | 01/09/1918 | 02/09/1918 |
| War Diary | Mory | 06/09/1918 | 06/09/1918 |
| War Diary | Adinper | 09/09/1918 | 09/09/1918 |
| War Diary | Vaulx | 09/09/1918 | 19/09/1918 |
| War Diary | Velu | 27/09/1918 | 27/09/1918 |
| War Diary | Havrincourt Wood | 29/09/1918 | 29/09/1918 |
| War Diary | Havrincourt | 30/09/1918 | 01/10/1918 |
| War Diary | Ribecourt | 02/10/1918 | 03/10/1918 |

| | | | |
|---|---|---|---|
| War Diary | Marcoing | 07/10/1918 | 11/10/1918 |
| War Diary | Boistrancourt | 17/10/1918 | 18/10/1918 |
| War Diary | Quievy | 23/10/1918 | 23/10/1918 |
| War Diary | Romeries | 24/10/1918 | 30/11/1918 |
| War Diary | Yvoir | 04/12/1918 | 04/12/1918 |
| War Diary | Pessoux Trisogne | 05/12/1918 | 05/12/1918 |
| War Diary | Bailonville | 06/12/1918 | 06/12/1918 |
| War Diary | Fronville Monville | 07/12/1918 | 07/12/1918 |
| War Diary | Pisenne | 09/12/1918 | 09/12/1918 |
| War Diary | Odeigne | 11/12/1918 | 11/12/1918 |
| War Diary | Prouedroux | 12/12/1918 | 12/12/1918 |
| War Diary | Beho | 13/12/1918 | 13/12/1918 |
| War Diary | Thommen | 14/12/1918 | 14/12/1918 |
| War Diary | Schomberg | 15/12/1918 | 15/12/1918 |
| War Diary | Kronenberg | 16/12/1918 | 16/12/1918 |
| War Diary | Blakenheim | 17/12/1918 | 17/12/1918 |
| War Diary | Mechernich | 18/12/1918 | 18/12/1918 |
| War Diary | Wollersheim | 19/12/1918 | 19/12/1918 |
| War Diary | Lendersdorf | 20/12/1918 | 31/12/1918 |
| Heading | 3 Div 40 Trench Mortar Bty 1915 July To 1916 Jan | | |
| War Diary | 42 Bde Ammn Col G 10 D.3.3 | 25/07/1915 | 25/07/1915 |
| War Diary | I 34a.6.6 Near Verbranden-Molen South Of Ypres | 28/07/1915 | 31/07/1915 |
| War Diary | Near Verbran-Denmolen South Of Ypres | 02/08/1915 | 02/08/1915 |
| War Diary | Verbrandenmolen | 05/08/1915 | 05/08/1915 |
| War Diary | Verbrandenmolen S Of Ypres | 05/08/1915 | 09/08/1915 |
| War Diary | ?War Vinhand In M | 10/08/1915 | 14/08/1915 |
| War Diary | Verbrandemolen | 16/08/1915 | 25/08/1915 |
| War Diary | Sanctuary Wood | 26/08/1915 | 10/10/1915 |
| War Diary | A.S. I 19 A 3.10 | 01/11/1915 | 07/11/1915 |
| War Diary | In Rest | 07/11/1915 | 10/11/1915 |
| War Diary | In Action | 11/11/1915 | 19/11/1915 |
| War Diary | A S | 29/11/1915 | 03/12/1915 |
| War Diary | In Field | 06/12/1915 | 18/12/1915 |
| War Diary | A.S. | 20/12/1915 | 31/12/1915 |
| Heading | 40 Trench Motar Bty Jan 1916 Vol VII | | |
| War Diary | In The Field | 02/01/1916 | 17/01/1916 |
| War Diary | Sanctuary Wood | 18/10/1915 | 24/10/1915 |
| War Diary | Sanctuary Wood | 11/10/1915 | 17/10/1915 |
| Heading | 3rd Division Divl. Artillery Trench Mortar Batts 1916 Mar-1916 Dec | | |
| Heading | 3rd Divisional Artillery. Z/3 Trench Mortar Battery (Late 308th) March 1916 | | |
| War Diary | Tournehem | 10/03/1916 | 31/03/1916 |
| Heading | 3rd Divisional. Artillery. 2/3 Trench Mortar Battery (late 308th) April 1916 | | |
| War Diary | Reninghelst | 01/04/1916 | 30/04/1916 |
| Heading | 3rd Divisional Artillery. 3rd Trench Mortar Batter July 1916 | | |
| War Diary | Bruay | 06/07/1916 | 06/07/1916 |
| War Diary | Chocques | 06/07/1916 | 07/07/1916 |
| War Diary | Doullen | 07/07/1916 | 07/07/1916 |
| War Diary | Vignacourt | 07/07/1916 | 08/07/1916 |
| War Diary | Raimeville | 08/07/1916 | 08/07/1916 |
| War Diary | Franmiller | 09/07/1916 | 10/07/1916 |
| War Diary | Albert | 10/07/1916 | 15/07/1916 |
| War Diary | In Action | 16/07/1916 | 20/07/1916 |

| | | | |
|---|---|---|---|
| War Diary | Albert | 21/07/1916 | 22/07/1916 |
| War Diary | In Action | 23/07/1916 | 23/07/1916 |
| War Diary | Albert | 24/07/1916 | 24/07/1916 |
| War Diary | In Action | 25/07/1916 | 26/07/1916 |
| War Diary | Millencourt | 27/07/1916 | 02/08/1916 |
| Heading | 3rd Divisional Artillery "X" "Y" "Z" Trench Mortar Batteries August 1916 | | |
| War Diary | Derwacourt | 01/08/1916 | 15/08/1916 |
| War Diary | Bray Sur Somme | 20/08/1916 | 27/08/1916 |
| War Diary | Noeux Les Mines | 28/08/1916 | 31/08/1916 |
| War Diary | Derwacourt | 01/08/1916 | 14/08/1916 |
| War Diary | Bray Sur Somme | 15/08/1916 | 28/08/1916 |
| War Diary | Woeux Les Mines | 29/08/1916 | 31/08/1916 |
| War Diary | Bray | 01/08/1916 | 01/08/1916 |
| War Diary | Dernancourt | 02/08/1916 | 30/08/1916 |
| Heading | 3rd Divisional Artillery. 3rd Trench Mortar Battery September 1916 | | |
| War Diary | In The Field | 01/09/1916 | 30/09/1916 |
| Heading | 3rd Divisional Artillery. 3rd Trench Mortar Battery October 1916 | | |
| War Diary | In The Field | 01/10/1916 | 31/10/1916 |
| Heading | 3rd Divisional Artillery. 3rd Trench Mortar Battery November 1916 | | |
| War Diary | Couaclles Au-Bois | 01/11/1916 | 30/11/1916 |
| Heading | 3rd Divisional Artillery. 3rd Trench Mortar Battery December 1916 | | |
| War Diary | Bus-En-Artois | 01/12/1916 | 31/12/1916 |
| Heading | 3rd Divisional Artillery. X/3 Trench Mortar Battery July 1916 | | |
| War Diary | | 01/07/1916 | 31/07/1916 |
| Heading | 3rd Divisional Artillery. Y/3 Trench Mortar Battery July 1916 | | |
| War Diary | | 01/07/1916 | 31/07/1916 |
| War Diary | Bray | 01/08/1916 | 01/08/1916 |
| War Diary | Dornancourt | 02/08/1916 | 02/08/1916 |
| War Diary | Bray | 15/08/1916 | 20/08/1916 |
| War Diary | Trones Wood | 21/08/1916 | 31/08/1916 |
| Heading | 3rd Divisional Artillery. Z/3 Trench Mortar Battery (Late 308th) July 1916 | | |
| War Diary | St. Comer | 01/07/1916 | 02/07/1916 |
| War Diary | Doulens | 03/07/1916 | 07/07/1916 |
| War Diary | Bois Des Tailles | 08/07/1916 | 09/07/1916 |
| War Diary | Bray | 11/07/1916 | 11/07/1916 |
| War Diary | Minden Post | 11/07/1916 | 21/07/1916 |
| War Diary | Bray | 22/07/1916 | 31/07/1916 |
| Heading | 3rd Divisional Artillery.V/3 Trench Mortar Battery July 1916 | | |
| War Diary | Audring | 02/07/1916 | 03/07/1916 |
| War Diary | Doulens | 03/07/1916 | 03/07/1916 |
| War Diary | Bourbon | 04/07/1916 | 04/07/1916 |
| War Diary | Daours | 05/07/1916 | 05/07/1916 |
| War Diary | Bois de Tailles | 07/07/1916 | 07/07/1916 |
| War Diary | Bray | 09/07/1916 | 30/07/1916 |
| Heading | 3rd Divisional Artillery. V/3 Trench Mortar Battery August 1916 | | |
| War Diary | Bray | 01/08/1916 | 01/08/1916 |

| | | | |
|---|---|---|---|
| War Diary | Dornancourt | 02/08/1916 | 02/08/1916 |
| War Diary | Bray | 15/08/1916 | 20/08/1916 |
| War Diary | Trones Wood | 21/08/1916 | 31/08/1916 |
| Heading | Division Ammunition Column 1914 Aug To 1919 Sept. Trench Mortar Bty's 1915 July To 1919 Feb | | |
| Heading | 3rd Divisional Divl. Artillery Trench Mortar Batteries 1918 Jan-1919 Feb | | |
| War Diary | Mory | 01/01/1918 | 08/02/1918 |
| War Diary | Boiry Becquerelle | 09/02/1918 | 28/02/1918 |
| Heading | 3rd Divisional Artillery. D.T.M.O. 3rd Divisional Trench Mortars March 1918 | | |
| War Diary | Boiry-Becquerelle | 01/03/1918 | 30/03/1918 |
| Heading | 3rd Divisional Artillery 3rd Divisional Trench Mortar Officer April 1918 | | |
| War Diary | Bavincourt | 01/04/1918 | 01/04/1918 |
| War Diary | Bieval | 02/04/1918 | 04/04/1918 |
| War Diary | Ruitz | 05/04/1918 | 11/04/1918 |
| War Diary | Noyelles | 12/04/1918 | 12/04/1918 |
| War Diary | Oblinghem | 13/04/1918 | 15/04/1918 |
| War Diary | Vendin-Lez-Bethune | 16/04/1918 | 22/04/1918 |
| War Diary | Chocques | 23/04/1918 | 07/08/1918 |
| War Diary | Bailleul-Les-Pernes | 08/08/1918 | 13/08/1918 |
| War Diary | Canettemont | 14/08/1918 | 14/08/1918 |
| War Diary | Humbercourt | 15/08/1918 | 26/08/1918 |
| War Diary | Pommier | 27/08/1918 | 31/08/1918 |
| Miscellaneous | 3rd Division | | |
| War Diary | Vertain | 01/11/1918 | 05/11/1918 |
| War Diary | Villers Pol | 09/11/1918 | 16/11/1918 |
| War Diary | Sclesmes | 19/11/1918 | 30/11/1918 |
| War Diary | Nideggen | 01/01/1919 | 28/02/1919 |
| Heading | Northern Division (Late 3rd Division) 3rd Divl Ammn Coln. Jan-Sep 1919 | | |
| War Diary | Lendersdorf (Germany) | 01/01/1919 | 28/02/1919 |
| Heading | War Diary of Northern Divisional Ammunition Column From 1st March 1919 To 31st March 1919 Volume 43 | | |
| War Diary | Brauweiler | 14/03/1919 | 31/03/1919 |
| Miscellaneous | Summary. | | |
| Miscellaneous | Northern Divisional Ammunition Column | | |
| War Diary | | 01/04/1919 | 01/04/1919 |
| War Diary | Brauweiler | 01/04/1919 | 28/04/1919 |
| Miscellaneous | Summary | | |
| War Diary | Brauweiler | 01/05/1919 | 31/05/1919 |
| Miscellaneous | Summary | | |
| War Diary | Brauweiler Germany | 03/06/1919 | 30/06/1919 |
| War Diary | Braulseiler Germany | | |
| War Diary | Brauweiler Germany | 01/07/1919 | 31/07/1919 |
| War Diary | Brauweiler Germany | | |
| War Diary | Brauweiler Germany | 01/08/1919 | 16/08/1919 |
| War Diary | Brauweiler Germany | | |
| War Diary | Brauweiler Germany | 09/09/1919 | 15/09/1919 |
| War Diary | Brauweiler | 18/09/1919 | 30/09/1919 |
| War Diary | Brauweiler Germany | | |
| Heading | 3rd Division War Diaries 3/Div. T.M. Battery. 1917January. to December | | |
| War Diary | Bus-En Artois | 01/01/1917 | 15/01/1917 |
| War Diary | St Ouen | 15/01/1917 | 30/01/1917 |

| | | | |
|---|---|---|---|
| War Diary | Boubers-Sur-Canche | 31/01/1917 | 28/02/1917 |
| War Diary | Arras | 01/03/1917 | 31/03/1917 |
| Miscellaneous | To 76th Infantry Bde | | |
| War Diary | Arras | 01/06/1917 | 30/06/1917 |
| War Diary | Simoncourt | 01/07/1917 | 01/07/1917 |
| War Diary | Bapaume | 02/07/1917 | 03/07/1917 |
| War Diary | Beaumetz-Lez-Cambrai | 04/07/1917 | 31/08/1917 |
| War Diary | Morchies | 01/09/1917 | 30/09/1917 |
| War Diary | Watou | 01/10/1917 | 14/10/1917 |
| War Diary | Etaples | 15/10/1917 | 15/10/1917 |
| War Diary | Bapaume | 16/10/1917 | 17/10/1917 |
| War Diary | Vaulx-Vraucourt | 19/10/1917 | 31/12/1917 |
| War Diary | Mory | 29/12/1917 | 31/12/1917 |

DIVISION AMMUNITION
COLUMN.
1914 AUG TO 1919 SEPT.
TRENCH MORTAR BTY'S
1915 JULY TO 1919 FEB

1402

## 3RD DIVISION
## DIVL ARTILLERY

3RD DIVL AMMUNITION COLUMN

AUG - DEC 1914

3rd Divisional Artillery.
-------------------

Copy of War Diary.

3rd DIVISIONAL AMMUNITION COLUMN R.F.A.

AUGUST 1914

3rd. Divl. Ammunition Column.

Vol. I.   5. VIII. 1914 — 30. VIII. 1914.

[There appears to be no available record for 31-VIII-1914 — 2-IX-1914 (both inclusive)]. †

The enclosed Diary is copied from the one at the R.H. & R.F.A Records at Woolwich.

† see appended note for Aug '14
(HCR)

Army Form C. 2118.

Diary of
III Divnl. Ammn. Coln.

True Copy – From

# WAR DIARY
or
## INTELLIGENCE SUMMARY
(Erase heading not required.)

Instructions regarding War Diaries and Intelligence Summaries are contained in F. S. Regs., Part II. and the Staff Manual respectively. Title Pages will be prepared in manuscript.

| Place | Date | Hour | Summary of Events and Information | Remarks and references to Appendices |
|---|---|---|---|---|
| HILSEA | Aug. 5th. '14. | 5.20 p.m. 1st day. | Received Order to Mobilise. The personnel for the formation of 3rd Divl. Ammn Col having been detailed in peace from the 3rd Res Bde R.F.A. PORTSMOUTH. The following offrs & men were allotted and as the latter became available, i.e. clothed & equipped, were despatched to BULFORD where the col. was formed.<br><br>Lt.Col. C.H.Ford   – comdg. ) From 3rd Res Bde R.F.A.,<br>Lt. R.M.Rendel   – Adjt.     ) Peace Establishment.<br>Maj. H.D.C. Ward – Comdg No. 1 Sectn. Detailed by War Office<br>Capt. O.Tritton     –          "         3   "    R.F.R.A.<br>  "   W.H.C.Despard –         "         "   2   "      do<br>  "   C.H.Mallock  –          "         "   4   "      do<br>Lt. J.D.C.Hawkins. Subaltern. 2   "      R.F.R.A.<br>  "   C.W. von Roemer   "       3   "      do    Special<br>2/"  G.B.R. Tease         "       3   "      do    Reserve.<br>  "   N.A. Browning-Teteson –  1   "      do<br>  "   S.M.de H.Whatton. S'altn. 2   "      do<br>  "   J.G.Montagu              "   4   "      do<br>  "   Voysey                     "   1   "      do Probr. )<br>1 W.O. 233gts., 11 Sgts. 2 Tptrs. – 32 Artificers – 505 o.r. = 568. | R.H. & R.F.A. Records.<br><br>Copy in possession of<br>N.F.J.B<br>Major 1917<br>13 .xii. |
| " | 6th | 5 pm. 1st day. | The Adjt & the W.O. (Sgt Maj M.W. Shepperd) left HILSEA with the first party for BULFORD. | |
| BULFORD | 7th 2nd day. | | The arrangement, during peace, of the personnel for the Column was that they shd arrive on 2 separate days in two batches, i.e. Regular Reservists (Section D). on the second day of mobilism, and the Special Reservists with their offrs on the 4th day.  Owing to congestion at HILSEA and withdrawal | |

Army Form C. 2118.

# WAR DIARY
or
## INTELLIGENCE SUMMARY

*(Erase heading not required.)*

Instructions regarding War Diaries and Intelligence Summaries are contained in F.S. Regs., Part II. and the Staff Manual respectively. Title Pages will be prepared in manuscript.

| Place | Date | Hour | Summary of Events and Information | Remarks and references to Appendices |
|---|---|---|---|---|
| BULFORD (contd). | August 7th (contd). | 2nd day | drawal of staff i.e. C.O. & Adjt & R.S.M. from HILSEA, the original scheme was not carried out, & drafts were sent to BULFORD indescriminately where they were sorted out and the column eventually rec'd most of its quota of Reservists as detailed above. | |
| " | 8th. 3rd | " | The equipment, vehicles, ammn & stores, were all stored in charge of the 4 Bdes. R.F.A. at BULFORD and sections of the Column were mobilised with their affiliated Bde i.e. No. 1 Section with 23rd Bde. No. 2 Sec with 42nd Bde. No. 3 Sec with 40th Bde, all 18 pdr Bdes. No. 4 Sec with 30th Bde howr. Bde. The Hvy portion of the latter Sec. was mobilised with 48 Hvy Bty R.G.A. at WOOLWICH. Owing to the Column hvg no permanent staff during peace - (except the Reservist Store- men) it was decided to wire for C.Os of Sectns to come at once. The first batch of N.C.Os & men (Reservists) also arrvd from HILSEA. | 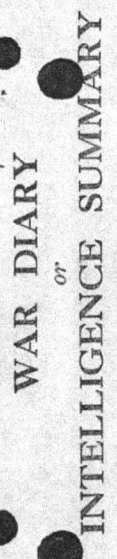 |
| " | 9th. 4th day. | " | Another draft arrvd, and the drawing of equipment commenced, each Sectn pitched camp in the vicinity of the Mobilisn Stores; troops were rationed & C by the affiliat- ed Bdes until provision was made by Sectn Commdrs. | |
| " | 10th. 5th | " | The C.O. arrvd and another large draft of men. The work of drawing stores, marking equipment was carried on from 6 am to 6 pm. Sectns hvg no Staff Sgts or Sgts the organizn &c suffered somewhat, as reservists (Corpls & Bom- brs) had to be promoted to Sgts, & an acting B.S.M. appntd. in each Sectn. Endless trouble was caused thro the Depot failing to see that each men had his A.B.64 on him prior to leaving HILSEA and it took days to sort the Pay books & their documents.<br>11th Aug. | |

Army Form C. 2118.

# WAR DIARY
## or
## INTELLIGENCE SUMMARY

*(Erase heading not required.)*

Instructions regarding War Diaries and Intelligence Summaries are contained in F. S. Regs., Part II. and the Staff Manual respectively. Title Pages will be prepared in manuscript.

| Place | Date | Hour | Summary of Events and Information | Remarks and references to Appendices |
|---|---|---|---|---|
| BULFORD | AUG. 11th '14. | 6th day | All offrs & men had now jnd & conducting parties were sent out for the horses, mostly to the Devon, Cornwall & Oxford shires, and were of a good type & stamp. | |
| " | 12th. | 7th " | All stores had been drawn & issued, horses teamed and a few wagons & teams went on driving drill. | |
| " | 13th. | 8th " | More horses arrvd, driving drill carried out, all rks. were kept busy night & day. | |
| " | 14th. | 9th " | All drills were now carried out in F.S.M.O. and reservists were settling down to their work. the M.O. jnd. Capt R.G.Bryden R.A.M.C. & an R.A.M.C. detachment of 4 men. 9 drivers A.S.C. also jnd for the supply and Baggage wagons. | |
| " | 15th. | 10th " | Column was to all intents and purposes ready for War. Surplus men were sent to R.A. details at the camp. BASE DETAILS, i.e. 1st re-enfts selected. Lt Lloyd Barrow 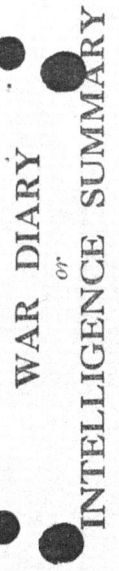 was inch charge of the latter. R.F.R.A. Anight march was practised, independently, by O.C. Sectns. Skeleton Drill, under th O.C. was also carried out. | |
| " | 16th. | 11th " | Men & horses were settling down to work. A parade of the whole Column to practise Tumn supply was held. Sections were greatly handicapped concerning the office routine, only 1 Pay Sgt being available, and no clerks were to be found amongst the men. | |
| " | 17th. | 12th " | Sections were busy drilling, orders for War explained. Standing orders of the Corps and Div read out. All promotions, except the 2S/Sgts with H.Q. were filled up in the Column from the Reservists N.C.Os & artificers. 18th. | |

2449 Wt. W14957/M90 750,000 1/16 J.B.C. & A. Forms/C.2118/12.

Army Form C. 2118.

# WAR DIARY
or
# INTELLIGENCE SUMMARY

*(Erase heading not required.)*

Instructions regarding War Diaries and Intelligence Summaries are contained in F.S. Regs., Part II and the Staff Manual respectively. Title Pages will be prepared in manuscript.

| Place | Date | Hour | Summary of Events and Information | Remarks and references to Appendices |
|---|---|---|---|---|
| BULFORD. | AUG. 18th '14. | 13th day. | All horses had been Malleined and, many N.C.Os & men were voluntarily inoculated for typhus. There was little sickness amongst men and horses whilst in camp. Orders rec'd to entrain at AMESBURY. On the evng of the 18th at 10 pm the col. commenced to entrain at AMESBURY Stn. Commencing with No. 1 Sectn. 9 trains were utilized, each sectn occupying 2 trains and H.Q. 1 train. Trains were despatched every 2 hrs & contd until 2 pm 19th Aug. The entraining was quickly carried out and without a cas. to the 580 offrs. & men. 727 horses and 113 vehicles. As each train arrvd at SOUTHAMPTON it was quickly detrained & embarkn. began. 4 trspts being required and all left at difft. times for an unknown Port. The embarkn was again carried out expeditiously & without a cas. | Establishment &c: H.Q. 1,2,3,sec. 4 Sec. Hr. Hy. Lt-  —  —  —  —  —  —  Lt.Col. 1. —  —  —  1. 1. Adjt. 1. —  —  —  1. 1. Maj.or Capt. —  1. —  —  —  —  Subs. —  2. —  —  —  —  W.O. 1. —  —  —  1. 1. S.Sgts. 2. —  —  —  1. 1. Sgts. —  3. —  —  1. 1. Cpls. —  2. —  —  1. 1. Brs. —  5. —  —  1. 1. Artif. —  9. —  —  4. 1. Grs. —  33. —  —  10. 6. Drs. —  93. —  —  42. 14. A.S.C. 1. 2. —  —  1. 1. R.A.M.C. 4. —  —  —  —  —  M.O. 1. —  —  —  —  —  V.O. 1. —  —  —  —  —  Horses. Riding. 12. 12. —  —  5. 3. Draught.LD 12. 178. —  —  79. 1. " H 4. 4. —  —  2. 28. Vehicles. Water carts. 2. —  —  —  12. 6. wagons. GS 2. 27. —  —  1. 1. supply wagons.1. 2. —  —  —  —  Maltese cart. 1. —  —  —  —  —  Total: 15 offrs. 563 men. 725 horses. 113 vehicles. |
| SOUTHAMPTON | 19th | | | |
| BOULOGNE. | 20th. | 4am. | Trspts arrvd off the French coast, & by 8 am were all berthed at BOULOGNE. Debarkn was quickly carried. Some horses were slung out, & others in boxes. (these same applies to embark) & again no cas. Sectns proceeded independently to a rest camp on the outskirts of the town. Hvy portion of No. 4 sec. 2nd at SOUTHAMPTON. | |
| " | 21st. | 9pm. | Sections left BOULOGNE in four separate trains commencing at m.night, & were railed via AMIENS, ST QUENTIN to VALENCIENNES, where the first train H.Q. & No. 4 sec. | |
| VALENCIENNES SULTAIN BAVAI. | 22nd. | 3pm. | arrvd at 5 pm. Detrained & mrchd abt 5 pm to concentrn area. Second Corps via SULTAIN, and arrvd at BAVAI at 10 pm. All sectns except No. 3 bivckd on roads leading | |
| BELGIUM. REIZ-de-BRELLE. | 23rd | 5am. | to town. Left at 5 am for the Battle area, held up by Second Div, passing into action. Sections proceeded to refilling pts at NORCHAIN. BLAGINES and GINLY. H.Q. | |
| MONS. MALPLAQUET SUR LE HON | | | remained on MALPLAQUET road. No. 3 not yet arrived. | |

Army Form C. 2118.

# WAR DIARY or INTELLIGENCE SUMMARY

*(Erase heading not required.)*

Instructions regarding War Diaries and Intelligence Summaries are contained in F. S. Regs., Part II. and the Staff Manual respectively. Title Pages will be prepared in manuscript.

| Place | Date | Hour | Summary of Events and Information | Remarks and references to Appendices |
|---|---|---|---|---|
| M O N S. | AUG. 23rd 1914. | 7 pm. | Battle contd all day. Orders recd to Park at SUR LE HON. No. 3 sectn arrvd & was sent up with ammn. | |
| BATTLE OF MONS | | | No. 1 Sectn. supplied 540 rds. 16 pr. & 40,000 rds. S.A.A. " 2 " " 1296 " " " " " " " " 3 " " 7 " " " " " " " " 4 " " 512 " " " 15,850 " " " " 4 " " 60 " 4.5. " " " 5 " | To refill Bde Ammn. Column. |
| | | | Nos 1 & 2 Sectns mvd out to supply ammn and part of No 4 sec. | |
| H O N. S.WAAST BAVAI | 24th. | 5 am. Noon. 4.30. | Mvd out at 5 am with No. 3 Sectn & part of No. 4 to BAVAI and ST WAAST, circled right around and came back to W of BAVAI. Found 15 wagons (empty) of No. 2 Sectn under Lts. Whatton & Hawkins. | |
| BATTLE OF MONS | | 5 pm. | No 3 Sectn mvd to Supply 40th Bde A.C got separated wagons with Capt Tritton going to BOUT LA HAUT, remdr of Sectn with Col. The portions of Nos. 1 & 2 Sectns. With Maj Ward and Capt Despard, had not yet rejnd the Col. No. 4 Sectn supplied ammn at QUEVI LA PETIT. | |
| JENLAIN R | " | 6 pm. | Orders recd to march to MAROILLES as arty and inf. Were now arrvg in our vicinity. Parked at in laager formation. | |
| | " | 8 pm. | Water scarce. Guards trebled. Saw Zepp. destroyed. | |
| LOUVIGNIES SALESCHES SOLESMES TROISVILLE BETRY | 25th | 2 am. | Marched via GOMEGNIES, VILLEREAU, POTELLE, LOUVIGNIES, RAUCOURT in the FOREST OF MORMAL and eventually arrived at SALESCHES, mvd after an hrs halt, via VENDE- GNIES, ordered to march on via ROMERIES SOLESMES, INCHY, TROISVILLE, and arrvd at BETRY, where the Col. parked with the exception of a few wagons that had not rejnd with Capt Despard. | |

26th.

Army Form C. 2118.

# WAR DIARY
## or
## INTELLIGENCE SUMMARY

*(Erase heading not required.)*

Instructions regarding War Diaries and Intelligence Summaries are contained in F. S. Regs., Part II. and the Staff Manual respectively. Title Pages will be prepared in manuscript.

| Place | Date | Hour | Summary of Events and Information | Remarks and references to Appendices |
|---|---|---|---|---|
| BATTLE OF "LE CATEAU" | AUGUST 26th 1914 | 4 am. | Marched out at 4 am. H.Q. to move to N of MARETZ Sections to refilling pts at BERTRY. CLARY. MALINCOURT & ELINCOURT. H.Q. parked at L'ALLOUETTE, where Park (No. 3) replenished Sectns. | |
| | | 5 pm. | Battle contd all day and was fiercest between 10 am & 3 pm. All ammn had been used up, part of No. 2 Section with empty wagons rejnd H.Q. Sections were busy all day and in some cases took amtn direct to the btties (Lt. Voysey & 2Lt Whatton). Recd orders to move to SERAIN. | |
| SERAIN. | | | Battle contd and our troops pressed back. A sectn of guns came into action S of the road to guard our rear and the Divl. Train. Road was blocked with all sorts of vehicles and the progress was slow. | |
| Nr SERAIN | | 7 pm. | Halted on side of road until 9.30 pm guiding wagons, troops, motors &c who were pouring down the road in confusion, collected abt 30 empty wagons of Nos 2 & 3 Sections. Coloured lights had now been erected to asst Bdes and Divns in re-assembling. | 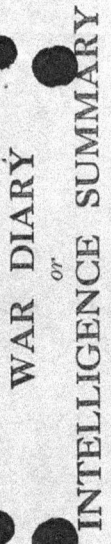 |
| " " | | 9.30pm. | Mvd at 9.30 pm. And the stream of vehicles that were mvg on the ROMAN RD to ESTREES. Marched till 2¾am arriving at ST QUENTIN. | of H.Q. now remained, the empty wagons |
| ST. QUEN- TIN. | 27th. | 2 am. | Bivckd on road S of town at 3 am, only the wagons had got separated during the night march. Some Cav. & E'grs bivckd close but had disappeared at 5 am when | |
| HAM. | | 5 am. | H.Q. mvd again twds HAM wh was reached abt 9 am. No news of the Sections of the Column. Wagons sent to supply ammn lost their way. 7 wagons of No. 1 & 12 of No. 2 Sec. could not be traced. Stores and ammn in some cases had to be abandoned to carry wounded men & the v. tired inf. | |

Army Form C. 2118.

# WAR DIARY
## or
## INTELLIGENCE SUMMARY

*(Erase heading not required.)*

Instructions regarding War Diaries and Intelligence Summaries are contained in F.S. Regs., Part II. and the Staff Manual respectively. Title Pages will be prepared in manuscript.

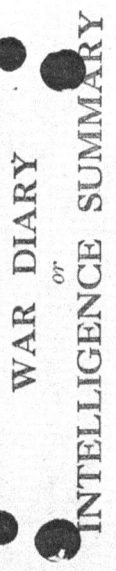

| Place | Date | Hour | Summary of Events and Information | Remarks and references to Appendices |
|---|---|---|---|---|
| S.QUENTIN HAM. | AUGUST 25th 1914 27th | 7pm. 2 am. 10pm. | No. 3 Sec. left MALINCOURT at 7 pm and marched to ST QUENTIN via BEAUREVOIR, ESTRESS, BELLINGLISE, PONT-FAYET - arrvg at ST Q., left at 6 pm & mrchd to HAM. Parked. Roads v. congested & many wagons got separated. | |
| LE CATEAU. BEAUREVOIR. | 26th 27th | 3.30 pm. 8 pm | No. 4 Sec. left BERTRY, reached BEAUREVOIR 8 pm. Ordered to Jn H.Q. mvd & mrchd all night. halted for 2 hrs. Mrchd to ST QUENTIN, arrvg at noon. | |
| GRICOURT ST QUENTIN HAM. | 27th | 7.30 a.m. 4.30 p.m. | Ordered to HAM by special road via ETREILLERS Germans were close and was ordered to gallop by a staff Reached HAM. | |
| LE CATEAU. | 26th 27th | 4 am. 2 pm. | No. 2 Sec. Left BERTRY & estbld refilling pt at CHARY & later at L'ALLOUETTE. Retired abt 4 pm to BEAUREVOIR, VERMAND wh was made a refilling pt. Capt Despard with 12 wagons did not rejn the main body of the col. until 30th Aug. at MALINGY nr VIC SUR AISNE. | |
| NOYON. CARLE PONT PONTOISE. | 28th | | Sections have now got split up & mvg by many routes twds COMPEIGNE thro' the forests of CARLE PONT & DE LAIGUE. Horses are getting done up thro' the constant mrchg since the 22nd Aug.. HQ and a few wagons arrvd at NOYON but mvd on to PONTOISE, & parked there. No 4 sect parts of No. 5 Sect & of No 1 Sect jnd & parked with H.Q. | |
| PONTOISE BAILLY. S.LEGER | 29th | | Left at 5.30 am for COMPEIGNE via the Forests of BOIS LE CARLE PONT and DELAIGUE arrvg at CHOISY AU BAC abt noon where HQ parked. Sectns or parts of them were enrvg thro' out the day and the Col. refmd except Maj Ward | |

Army Form C. 2118.

# WAR DIARY
## or
## INTELLIGENCE SUMMARY

*(Erase heading not required.)*

Instructions regarding War Diaries and Intelligence Summaries are contained in F. S. Regs., Part II. and the Staff Manual respectively. Title Pages will be prepared in manuscript.

| Place | Date | Hour | Summary of Events and Information | Remarks and references to Appendices |
|---|---|---|---|---|
| | AUGUST 29th 1914 (contd) | | Maj Ward with 11 wagons of No. 1 Sectn - 12 wagons of No. 2 Sectn with Capt Despard and 4 wagons of No. 3 Sectn. Many stragglers of all Corps had collected or had been picked up by wagons. Ammn & stores were drawn from COMPIEGNE. | |
| CHOISYAU BAC. | 30th. | 1pm. | Left at 1 pm recd sudden orders to move & mrchd. via COMPEIGNE FOREST to MONTIGNY, where we parked for | |
| MONTIGNY. | | 8 pm. | the night. No. 2 Sectn wagons rejnd. | |

2449 Wt. W14957/M90 750,000 1/16 J.B.C. & A. Forms/C.2118/12.

3rd Divisional Artillery.

ORIGINAL WAR DIARY.

3rd DIVISIONAL AMMUNITION COLUMN R.F.A.

AUGUST 1914.

# WAR DIARY
## or
## INTELLIGENCE SUMMARY.
*(Erase heading not required.)*

Army Form C. 2118.

3rd Div Am Column

Page (1)

| Hour, Date, Place | Summary of Events and Information | Remarks and references to Appendices |
|---|---|---|
| 5.45pm 5th August/14 Aldershot | Received order to Mobilize | |
| 5.25pm 6th " " | T.W.O. left to join H.Q. 3 Div A.C. at Bulford. | |
| 11.30pm 6th " " Bulford | 1st Rendal Adj't & B.S.M. left in charge of a party of men for Bulford. | |
| 5pm 7th " " " | Received 259 men from 3rd Res. Brigade RFA Aldershot | |
| 2pm 8th " " " | " 200 men " " " " | |
| 5pm 8th " " " | o/c Sections arrived. | |
| 7pm 9th " " " | Subalterns & about 100 men arrive. | |
| 9am 9th " " " | Commenced drawing equipment &c from Mob Store | |
| 6am 10th " " " | " " " & ammn to respective Camps | |
| 6am 11th " " " | Drawing wagons & ammn | |
| 6am 12th " " " | Organising Sections | |
| 6am 13th " " " | Commenced to Receive Horses | |
| 6am 14th " " " | Receiving and Taming Horses | |
| 6am 15th " " " | Marking, Bitting, Harness & Equipment – Driving Drill afternoon | |
| 6am 16th " " " | Driving Drill – Skeleton C/o's Scheme | |
| 9am 17th " " " | Field Service Marching Order. C/o's Scheme repeated. | |
| 9am 17th " " " | The whole of the 3rd DAC paraded in F.S.M.O. practised ammn | |
| 9am 17th " " " | Supply – Night March at night. | |
| 9am 18th " " " | Sections again paraded in F.S.M.O. | |
| 9am 18th " " " | G.O. Inspected the whole of the 3rd Div A.C. in F.S.M.O. ready for War – Moved to Inkel Bn once. | Unit ready for War |

# WAR DIARY or INTELLIGENCE SUMMARY

3rd Div. Am. Col  Army Form C. 2118.
Page 2

| Hour, Date, Place | Summary of Events and Information | Remarks and references to Appendices |
|---|---|---|
| 19-8-14 Bulford | No 1 Section entrained in two trains at Midnight | |
| 20.8.14 " | No 2 " do " at 1 am | |
| " " " | No 3 " do " at 3 am | |
| " " " | No 4 " one train " 5 am | |
| " " " | H.Q.rs " one train " 11 am | |
| | There were no casualties & entraining was quickly carried out – average time 30 minutes. Troops proceeded to Southampton, and embarked on various transports. | |
| 20th August 1914 | No 1 Section & ½ of No 2 Sec on "Manchester Importer" | |
| | No 3 Section, ½ of No 2 & ½ of No 4 Sec on "Roumanian" | |
| | H.Q. & ½ Heavy Potion & No 4 Section on "City of Chester" | |
| 21-8-14 Boulogne | Ships arrived at Dawn off the Coast of France. Eventually arrived at Boulogne, disembarked & proceeded to a rest Camp, out in the Suburbs | |

Army Form C. 2118.

J. Dur an Col
(3)

# WAR DIARY
## or
## INTELLIGENCE SUMMARY
(Erase heading not required.)

Instructions regarding War Diaries and Intelligence Summaries are contained in F.S. Regs., Part II. and the Staff Manual respectively. Title pages will be prepared in manuscript.

| Hour, Date, Place | Summary of Events and Information | Remarks and references to Appendices |
|---|---|---|
| 21 Aug 1/4. BOULOGNE | Entrained whole BTTS. in 8 trains. | |
| 22nd Aug. VALENCIENNES | Arrived at various times during the day. Marched to BAVAI the same day after entraining and bivouacked, with exception of No 3 Section which went to St WAAST | |
| 23rd Aug. BAVAI NOIRCHAIN HON | Left BAVAI. Marched to RIEZ DE LEREUE. Section replenished Ammunition Column (Bde) during the day. Bivouacked at HON, after returning from NOIRCHAIN | Ammunition supplied to troops of IIIrd Div. operating near MONS  do do do NOIRCHAIN |
| 24th Aug. St WAAST AMPHROIPRET BAVAI | Left Bivouac at 8 a.m. arrived St WAAST about noon. March to AMPHROIPRET via BAVAI | |
| 25th Aug. VENDEGIES TROISVILLES BUSIGNY BERTRY | Left Bivouac at 2 a.m. arrived VENDEGIES 7 a.m. Left at 11 a.m. Arrived BUSIGNY TROISVILLES in the afternoon and went into bivouac W. of BERTRY. | Preceded the Division which was slowly falling back |
| 26 Aug. ♯ELINCOURT | Left BERTRY at 4 am and whole column parked at L'ALOUETTE just S. of ELINCOURT during the morning | |

(9 29 6) W 3332 —1107  100,000  10/13  H W V    Forms/C. 2118/10.

# WAR DIARY
## or
## INTELLIGENCE SUMMARY.
(Erase heading not required.)

Army Form C. 2118.

of 3rd Div: Am: Col

Instructions regarding War Diaries and Intelligence Summaries are contained in F.S. Regs., Part II. and the Staff Manual respectively. Title pages will be prepared in manuscript.

| Hour, Date, Place | Summary of Events and Information | Remarks and references to Appendices |
|---|---|---|
| 26 Aug. MAUNCOURT, FLINCOURT, CLARY, MARETZ | That morning sections were replenished with ammunition from 2nd Div Am Park and at later from 3rd Div. Park. Sections supplied Bde Am Col with ammunition at MAUNCOURT, CLARY, ELINCOURT, and MARETZ | On this day both III" & IV" Bde - ie vans were supplied with ammunition practically the whole of the ammunition left of His Grand ammunition & III" Reserve Park Bde sent to the rescue of the Army Corps - on three occasions Park delivered at the Army Brass ford column vehicles & I HAM KINS - 2nd VOYSEY. WHATTON |
| SERAM | That night Head Quarters proceeded to SERAM and went South about 1 mile and parked for about [illegible] hour being when the column collected partially about | |
| ESTREES | for ESTREES when the column collected partially about 9.30 pm. Left ESTREES that night and arrived just | |
| 27 Aug. ST QUENTIN | S of ST. QUENTIN at 2 a.m. next day. Left St QUENTIN at 5 a.m. Head Quarters leading for | In the vicinity of HAM 8 G.S. wagons were emptied & used to convey wounded from the rear guard troops under the orders of G O C IX Inf. Brigade. |
| HAM NOYON | NOYON passing through HAM and arriving at 4 pm. Ammunition being supplied by sections near HAM, went into | |
| SEMPIGNY | bivouac at SEMPIGNY. Head Quarters only night, section coming south by various routes next day | |

Army Form C. 2118.

Instructions regarding War Diaries and Intelligence Summaries...

WAR DIARY
or
INTELLIGENCE SUMMARY.

Army Form C. 2118.

5" Divi Am Col (5)

WAR DIARY
or
INTELLIGENCE SUMMARY.
(Erase heading not required.)

| Hour, Date, Place | Summary of Events and Information | Remarks and references to Appendices |
|---|---|---|
| 28 Aug. CHOISIS AU BAC | Left SEMPIGNY (HdQrs only) at 9 a.m. and arrived at CHOISIS AU BAC at 2 p.m. and went into Bivouac. | |
| 29. Aug. CHOISIS AU BAC | Remained at CHOISIS AU BAC and joined by sections from various parts of the country. | |
| 30 Aug. MONTIGNY | Left CHOISIS AU BAC at 1 p.m. march to MONTIGNY where we arrived 8 p.m. | |
| 31 Aug. LEVIGNEN | Left MONTIGNY at 5 a.m. with orders to march to VEZ but were diverted to VIC SUR AISNE diverted to LEVIGNEN where we arrived about 10 p.m. | |

3rd Divisional Artillery.

---

3rd DIVISIONAL AMMUNITION COLUMN R.F.A.

SEPTEMBER 1914.

Army Form C 2118.

# WAR DIARY
or
## INTELLIGENCE SUMMARY.
*(Erase heading not required.)*

Instructions regarding War Diaries and Intelligence Summaries are contained in F. S. Regs., Part II. and the Staff Manual respectively. Title pages will be prepared in manuscript.

| Place | Date | Hour | Summary of Events and Information | Remarks and references to Appendices |
|---|---|---|---|---|
| BOUILLANCY | 1st Sept | | Left LEVIGNEN at 6.30 am marched to BOUILLANCY, arrived there about 10 am and parked. Left the park about 2 pm and arrived BREGY 4 pm. where we bivouaced for the night. | |
| BREGY | | | | |
| MONTIGNY | 2nd Sept | | Left BREGY 1.30 a.m for MONTIGNY where we arrived at 5 am. | |
| TRILBARDOU | | | Left at 5 pm for LESCHES, on arrival at TRILBARDOU Bridge | |
| CRECY | | | returned to GRANDE LOGE FMS via CRECY and LA HAUTE | |
| LA HAUTE MAISON | | | MAISON. Arrived in bivouac 1 a.m. | |
| GRANDE LOGE FMS | 3rd Sept | | | |

Army Form C. 2118.

# WAR DIARY
## or
## INTELLIGENCE SUMMARY.
(Erase heading not required.)

Instructions regarding War Diaries and Intelligence
Summaries are contained in F. S. Regs., Part II.
and the Staff Manual respectively. Title pages
will be prepared in manuscript.

| Hour, Date, Place | Summary of Events and Information | Remarks and references to Appendices |
|---|---|---|
| 3ʳᵈ Sept. GRANDE LOGE FRM LA BARDE | Left at 5pm. arrived in Bivouac near LA BARDE and remained there the night. | |
| 4ᵗʰ Sept. PARIS GUERARD MONTCERF LA HOUSSAYE CHATEAU DES BOULAYES | Left 11 a.m. and marched for the CHATEAU DES BOULAYES near TOURNON via PARIS and GUERARD - MONTCERF - LA HOUSSAYE. arriving at 11.30 pm. | |
| 5ᵗʰ Sept. CHATRES LIVERDY RETAL VILLERAYEN | Left CHATEAU DES BOULAYES about 11 a.m. for VILLERAYEN via CHATRES - LIVERDY and RETAL arriving about 3pm. | |
| 6ᵗʰ Sept. CHAMPROSE | Left at 5pm and marched for CHAMPROSE arriving at 6pm. | |
| 7ᵗʰ Sept. LIVERDY LUMIGNY | Left at 12.15 p.m. for LUMIGNY via LIVERDY and CHATRES and MARLES. Arrived 4 p.m. | |
| 8ᵗʰ Sept. COULOMMIERS ST PIERRE BELLEVUE | Left 8 a.m. for COULOMMIERS arrived 12 noon at NEW MARKET. ST PIERRE BELLEVUE | |

Army Form C. 2118.

# WAR DIARY
## or
## INTELLIGENCE SUMMARY.
*(Erase heading not required.)*

Instructions regarding War Diaries and Intelligence Summaries are contained in F.S. Regs., Part II. and the Staff Manual respectively. Title pages will be prepared in manuscript.

| Hour, Date, Place | Summary of Events and Information | Remarks and references to Appendices |
|---|---|---|
| 8th Sept. LES BROSSES | Left ST PIERRE at 6 p.m. and arrived near LES BROSSES at 8 p.m. | |
| 9th Sept. REBAIS | Left 8.30 a.m. arrived at REBAIS at 11 a.m. | |
| 10th Sept. NANTEUIL | Left at 10 a.m. marched by ORLY, BUSSIERES and arrived NANTEUIL at 1.30 p.m. During the night 6 guns captured by the Lincoln Regt. were fetched and loaded on motor lorries and sent to Rail head. | |
| 11th Sept. VEUILLY MONTREUIL MERY DAMMARD | Left NANTEUIL at 10 a.m. via VEUILLY and MONTREUIL — MERY and arrived at 5 p.m. at DAMMARD at 5 p.m. | |
| 12th Sept. NEUILLY OULCHY LA VILLE GRAND ROZOY | Left at 1 p.m. and marched via NEUILLY — OULCHY LA VILLE — to GRAND ROZOY arriving 5 p.m. | |

[signature] Capt. R.F.A.
Adjutant 3rd Div. Am. Col.

Army Form C. 2118.

# WAR DIARY
## or
## INTELLIGENCE SUMMARY.
*(Erase heading not required.)*

Instructions regarding War Diaries and Intelligence Summaries are contained in F. S. Regs., Part II. and the Staff Manual respectively. Title pages will be prepared in manuscript.

| Hour, Date, Place | Summary of Events and Information | Remarks and references to Appendices |
|---|---|---|
| 13 Sept. BRAINE | Left GRAND ROZOY at 1 p.m. forming BRAINE at 5 p.m. | |
| 14. | | |
| 15. | | |
| 16. | | |
| 17. | | |
| 18. | | |
| 19. | | |
| 20. BRAINE | | |
| 21. | | |
| 22. | | |
| 23. | | |
| 24. | | |
| 25. | | |
| 26. | | |
| 27. | | |
| 28. | | |
| 29. | | |
| 30. LESGES | Marched to LESGES and went into billets | |

Capt. R.F.A.
Am. Col.
Adjutant 3rd. Div. Am. Col.

3rd Divisional Artillery.

3rd DIVISIONAL AMMUNITION COLUMN R.F.A.

OCTOBER 1914.

Army Form C. 2118.

# WAR DIARY or INTELLIGENCE SUMMARY.

(Erase heading not required.)

Instructions regarding War Diaries and Intelligence Summaries are contained in F. S. Regs., Part II. and the Staff Manual respectively. Title pages will be prepared in manuscript.

| Hour, Date, Place | Summary of Events and Information | Remarks and references to Appendices |
|---|---|---|
| 1st October 1914. | In billets at LESGES. | |
| 2nd " | } | |
| 3rd CHOUY | Left at 6 p.m. and marched to CHOUY via ARCY and GRAND ROZOY to billets at 3 am. | |
| 4th LA FERTÉ MILON | Left CHOUY at 8 p.m. and marched to LA FERTÉ MILON arriving about 11 p.m. in billets | |
| 5th CREPY | Left Ferté at 7.30 p.m. for CREPY arriving at 2.30 a.m. in billets. | |
| 6th CREPY EN VALOISE | Remained in billets in CREPY | |
| 7th VERBERIE | Left at 11 a.m. marched to VERBERIE and went into bivouac. | |
| 8th VERBERIE PONTREMY | Left VERBERIE 4 a.m. marched to LE MEUX and entrained arriving at PONT REMY at 5 p.m. Du- entrained and left at 9 p.m. Arrived LE PLESSIEL | |
| 9th LE PLESSIEL | at 1.30 am 9th | |

Adjutant 3rd Div. Amm. Co[l]

Capt. R.F.A.

Army Form C. 2118.

# WAR DIARY
## or
## INTELLIGENCE SUMMARY.
*(Erase heading not required.)*

Instructions regarding War Diaries and Intelligence Summaries are contained in F.S. Regs., Part II. and the Staff Manual respectively. Title pages will be prepared in manuscript.

| Hour, Date, Place | Summary of Events and Information | Remarks and references to Appendices |
|---|---|---|
| 10. Oct/14 LePLESSIEL | Left at 4 a.m. and march to Lillers at INCOURT arriving there about noon. | |
| INCOURT | | |
| 11.Oct/14 SAINS. | Left INCOURT at 8 a.m. marched to SAINS arriving at 12.30 p.m. | |
| 12. Oct/14 AUCHEL | Left SAINS at 8 a.m. marched via AUCHEL to ALLOUAGNE arriving at 11 a.m. | |
| ALLOUAGNE | | |
| 13. Oct/14 LOCON | Left at 2.15 p.m. arrived LOCON at about 5 p.m. Remained in billets in LOCON | |
| 14 Oct/14 LOCON | | |
| 15 Oct/14 LOCON | | |
| 16 Oct/14 | | |
| 17 Oct/14 | | |
| 18 Oct/14 | | |
| 19 | | |
| 20 | | |
| 21 | | |
| 22 | | |
| 23 | | |

Capt. R.F.A.
Capt. Am. Col.
Adjutant 3rd. Div. Am. Col.

Army Form C. 2118.

# WAR DIARY
## or
## INTELLIGENCE SUMMARY.
(Erase heading not required.)

Instructions regarding War Diaries and Intelligence Summaries are contained in F. S. Regs., Part II. and the Staff Manual respectively. Title pages will be prepared in manuscript.

| Hour, Date, Place | Summary of Events and Information | Remarks and references to Appendices |
|---|---|---|
| Oct 24. LOCON | | |
| 25. — | | |
| 26. — | | |
| 27. — | | |
| 28. — | | |
| 29. L'EPINETTE | Left LOCON at 10.30 a.m. for L'EPINETTE | |
| 30. L'EPINETTE | Left L'EPINETTE at 10 a.m. and marched into Billets at LESTREM. | |
| 31. LESTREM | | |

3rd Divisional Ammunition Column

3RD DIVISIONAL AMMUNITION COLUMN R.F.A.

NOVEMBER 1914.

# WAR DIARY or INTELLIGENCE SUMMARY.

Army Form C. 2118.

(Erase heading not required.)

Instructions regarding War Diaries and Intelligence Summaries are contained in F.S. Regs., Part II. and the Staff Manual respectively. Title pages will be prepared in manuscript.

| Hour, Date, Place | Summary of Events and Information | Remarks and references to Appendices |
|---|---|---|
| Nov 1914, LESTREM | | |
| 13. 1914 LESTREM | | |
| 14." FERME DU PRINCE | Marched to billets at FERME DU PRINCE via LA GORGUE and ESTAIRES arriving at 8 p.m. | |
| 15." VIEUX BERQUIN | Left at 10 a.m. and marched to VIEUX BERQUIN via BOULEU arriving at noon | |
| 16: 17: 18: ditto | | |
| 19: RENINGHELST | Left at 7.30 a.m. for RENINGHELST via BAILLEUL and LOCRE (thus crossing) into BELGIUM arriving 11.30 a.m. | |
| 20 BERTHEN | Left at 6 p.m. for BERTHEN arriving there between the hours of 7 a.m. 21.xi. and 5 p.m. | |
| 30 BERTHEN | | |

Capt. R.F.A.
Adjutant 3rd Div. Ammn. Col.

3rd Divisional Artillery.

----------

3rd DIVISIONAL AMMUNITION COLUMN R.F.A.

DECEMBER 1914.

# WAR DIARY or INTELLIGENCE SUMMARY.

Army Form C. 2118.

| Hour, Date, Place | Summary of Events and Information | Remarks and references to Appendices |
|---|---|---|
| Dec 14th BERTHEN | Still at BERTHEN. | |
| 14th New MONT NOIR | Moved at 6 a.m. to billets near MONT NOIR arriving there about 7 a.m. | |
| 15 " " | | |
| 16 " " | | |
| 17th BERTHEN | Marched at 10.30 a.m. for BERTHEN. | |
| 17th to 29th BERTHEN | | |
| 30th St JANS CAPPEL | Marched at 8.30 a.m. for St JANS CAPPEL & moved into Billets there | |
| 31st " " | | |
| 1915 | | |
| 1 to 31 January | In Billets | |
| (St JANS CAPPEL) | | |

Capt. R.F.A.
3rd Div. Am. Col.

Index..........................

## SUBJECT.

3rd DIV

| No. | Contents. | Date. |
|---|---|---|
| | R.F.A. — Ammunition Column, — War Diary, Jan - Dec, 1915 | |

Copied from Dec 1914 Diary

3rd Div. Amm. Col.

# WAR DIARY
## or
## INTELLIGENCE SUMMARY.

Army Form C. 2118.

January 1915.

(Erase heading not required.)

| Place | Date | Hour | Summary of Events and Information | Remarks and references to Appendices |
|---|---|---|---|---|
| St Jans Cappell | 1915 1st to 3rd Jan | | In Billets | |

121/4816

3rd Div'l Amm "Col"

Vol III

1st FEB to 31st MARCH
1915

1.2.15 to 31.3.15

Army Form C. 2118.

# WAR DIARY
## or
## INTELLIGENCE SUMMARY
(Erase heading not required.)

3rd Div Ammn Col

| Hour, Date, Place | Summary of Events and Information | Remarks and references to Appendices |
|---|---|---|
| 1915<br>1st to 28th February.<br>St JANS CAPPEL | In Billets and Shelters.<br>The following officers joined during the month<br>2/Lt J.S. GREEN from 40th Bde RFA A.C. on 18th.<br>2/Lt D.M.L. JOHNSON from Base on 20-2-15<br>The undermentioned officers left during the month<br>2/Lt F.C. Muskell to 30th Brigade AC 4th " " .<br>" F.S GREEN to 40" " . on 5th<br>" D.M.L JOHNSON to 42" " 23rd<br>Major C S'L HAWKES to RA II Div 27th<br><br>West Capt RFA<br>Comdg 3 Div A.C. | HEAD QUARTERS<br>2 APR 1915<br>3 DIV AMMN. COL |

Army Form C. 2118.

# WAR DIARY
## or
## INTELLIGENCE SUMMARY.
*(Erase heading not required.)*

N.d.g.t
3rd Div Am Col

| Hour, Date, Place | Summary of Events and Information | Remarks and references to Appendices |
|---|---|---|
| 1915<br>1st & 31st March<br>St. JANS. CAPPEL | In Billets and Shelters.<br><br>A detachment from No 4 Section (Heavy Potion) consisting of 6 NCO's 7 men - 8 horses and 2 wagons with 60 pdr Ambr. left to join 31st. Heavy Bty A.C. (4th Div) on 7½.<br><br>No 3 Section (1st) left for OUDERDOM. (Belgium) as advanced Section on 25½.<br><br>The undermentioned officers Joined and left during the month<br><br>Joined.  Bt. Col A.J. HUGHES to command the Column from Base 5th<br>Lt. A.E. Brown (RAMC) as medical officer, from 7 Janr 25th<br>YLt. A (C.S.) Fox from Base 23rd<br>Lt. D.M Hunter (RAMC) Sick to Base 19th<br>YLt. A Fox to 42 Brigade RFA. 26th | [stamp: HEAD QUARTERS 3 APR 1915 3 DIV. AMMN. COL] |

A.J. Hughes Colonel R.A
Comdg 3 Div Am Col

(9 29 6) W 4141-463 100,000 9/14 HWV  Forms/C. 2118/10

121/5255

3rd Dist Annual Conv^n
Votes 1-30-45

APRIL 1915

Army Form C. 2118.

# WAR DIARY
## INTELLIGENCE SUMMARY.
*(Erase heading not required.)*

Instructions regarding War Diaries and Intelligence Summaries are contained in F.S. Regs, Part II. and the Staff Manual respectively. Title pages will be prepared in manuscript.

| Hour, Date, Place | Summary of Events and Information | Remarks and references to Appendices |
|---|---|---|
| **April 1915** | | |
| 1st to 8th St Jans Cappel (France) Ouderdom (Belgium) | Head Quarters Nos 1 and 2 Sections and part of No 4 Section at St JANS CAPPEL. No 3 Section and part of No 4 Section at OUDERDOM. The Remaining portion of the Heavy portion of No 4 Sec. left to join 148th Heavy Bty Ammn Column on 8th. The party consisted of 19 N.Co.s & men (R.G.A.) 24 Horses and 5 wagons G.S. | |
| 1st April | Capt W.H.C. DESPARD R.F.R.A. Comdg 2 Sec. was sent to Base Sick on the 1st | |
| 9th April | Orders Received to Move to Vicinity of BERTHEN — WESTOUTRE Road. Marched at 1-30 p.m. No 3 & 4 Sections occupied farms near WESTOUTRE (Belgium) HdQrs & No 2 Sections towards BOESCHEPPE (France). | |
| 10th to 30th April Westoutre Boescheppe Reninghelst | No 3 Section moved from OUDERDOM to RENINGHELST on 12/4/15. No 4 Section Moved to Near RENINGHELST on the remaining portion of No 4 Section (6 wagons) Moved out to RENINGHELST on 21st APRIL. 15. Captain C.H. MALLOCK assumed command of No 2 Section on 23rd April — Lieut C Walker left to Join No 27 Ammunition Park on 22nd April — Lieut A IBBITSON assumed command of No 4 Section on 23rd APRIL. | 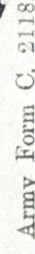 J/hy/hy Colonel 1st Comdg. 3rd Div A.C. |

Forms/C.2115/10
(9 29 6) W 4141—463 100,000 9/14 HWV

# WAR DIARY or INTELLIGENCE SUMMARY.

*(Erase heading not required.)*

**APRIL 1915**

Army Form C. 2118.

*Instructions regarding War Diaries and Intelligence Summaries are contained in F.S. Regs., Part II. and the Staff Manual respectively. Title pages will be prepared in manuscript.*

| Hour, Date, Place | Summary of Events and Information | Remarks and references to Appendices |
|---|---|---|
| April 1915 | | |
| 10th to 30th WESTOUTRE BOESCHEPE RENING HELST. | Heavy attack on Drench and Canadians on 22nd Column warned to prepare for heavy expenditure of ammunition - | |
| | 23rd APRIL. Received orders to prepare to MOVE up to RENING HELST. | |
| | Battle continued from 22nd to 29th April - | |
| | Lieut H E BROWN reported to Field Ambulance (RAMC) on relief by Lieut W K Russell RAMC (SR) from 7 Field Ambulance on 14th April - | |
| | No abnormal expenditure of ammunition during the month. | |
| | A. J. Hughes Colonel AJK | |
| | Comdg 3rd Divn Am Col | |

## "A" Form.
### MESSAGES AND SIGNALS.

Army Form C. 2121
No. of Message _____

| Prefix | Code | m. | Words | Charge | | Recd. at | m. |
|---|---|---|---|---|---|---|---|
| Office of Origin and Service Instructions | | | Sent At _____ m. To _____ By _____ | | *HEAD QUARTERS* This message is on a/c of APR 1915 Service. (Signature of "Franking Officer.") | Date _____ From _____ By _____ | |

**TO** { D.A. Ammn Col

| Sender's Number. | Day of Month. | In reply to Number | AAA |
|---|---|---|---|
| SC 291 | 22 | | |

Heavy attacks against French on Left of Canadians this evening aaa French retired causing withdrawal of Canadian left towards WIELTJE aaa Two reserve battalions from VLAMERTINGHE sent up aaa possible German concentration at MENIN reported indicating possible attack against 2nd Corps aaa all units should show increased vigilance aaa Nos 3 and 4 Sections informed.

From: 3rd D A
Place:
Time: 10.30 p.m.

The above may be forwarded as now corrected.  (Z)   [signature]

Censor. Signature of Addressor or person authorised to telegraph in his name.

* This line should be erased if not required.

"A" Form.  Army Form C. 2121.
## MESSAGES AND SIGNALS.

TO: All Ammn Col.

Sender's Number: A 262
Day of Month: 23

AAA

All units have been ordered to fill up with ammunition at once aaa Be prepared for heavy expenditure aaa Repeated 3rd Secn.

From
Place: 3rd Div Arty.
Time:

Major

3rd Div. Amm'n Col'n

WD IV 1 – 31.5.15

# WAR DIARY

**5th Div Ammn Column**

Army Form C. 2118.

## INTELLIGENCE SUMMARY.

*(Erase heading not required.)*

| Hour, Date, Place | Station. | Summary of Events and Information | Remarks and references to Appendices |
|---|---|---|---|
| 1915 May | | 1st to 30th May. | |
| WESTOUTRE (B) No. 1 Sec | M. WESTOUTRE | 1st to 29th May: Near BUSSEBOOM 30/31st | HEAD QUARTERS 2 JUN 15 DIV. AMMN. COL. |
| BOESCHEPPE (F) 2. | — do — | 1st to 5th — " — RENINGHELST 6/30th | |
| RENINGHELST (B) 3. | M. BOESCHEPPE | 1st to 5th — " — Near BOESCHEPPE 6/30th | |
| 4. | RENINGHELST | 1st to 5th — " — Near BOESCHEPPE 6/30th | |
| | — do — | 1st to 30th | |
| 30th May 6 am | YPRES Salient | No 3 Section was Advanced Section, was relieved by No 2 Section on 5th. No 1 Section Relieved No 2 Section on 30th as Advanced Section on the Move & 3rd Division to YPRES Salient | |
| 31st May 6 am | | No. 4 Section (Now 2) consisting of 1 Officer, 45 NCOs + men, 9 wagons, 52 Horses were transferred to the 5th Div Ammn Column with effect from 31st May 1915. | |
| 31st May 3 P.M. | | H. Qr. Nos 2 & 3 Sections moved at 3 pm on 31st May into Bivouac on the RENINGHELST - POPERINGHE Road, arriving about 4 pm. | |
| POPERINGHE (B) | | | |
| BUSSEBOOM (B) | | No 1 Section moved to m. BUSSEBOOM on 30th May. The Advanced Section Supplies all ammunition to Brigade Ammn Cols except in case of great urgency. *(continued)* | |

Army Form C. 2118.

# WAR DIARY
## or
## INTELLIGENCE SUMMARY.
(Erase heading not required.)

3rd Div Ammn Col

Continued

Instructions regarding War Diaries and Intelligence Summaries are contained in F.S. Regs., Part II. and the Staff Manual respectively. Title pages will be prepared in manuscript.

| Hour, Date, Place | Summary of Events and Information | Remarks and references to Appendices |
|---|---|---|
| May 1915. 2nd | Slight effects were felt of the enemy's gas attack on the morning of the 2nd. There was no unusual expenditure of Ammn during the month, except on night 30/31st 1100 rounds were expended. | HEAD QUARTERS 2 JUN 1915 DIV. AMMN. COY |
| | Changes in Officers during the Month | |
| 2.5.15 | Captain N.C.T. PARKER from Base, to Command N° 3 Section | |
| 2.5.15 | " " R Maclean " " " N° 4 " | |
| 22.5.15 | " " H.A.L. ROSE from Adjt 3 DAC to 30th Brigade RFA | |
| 22.5.15 | " " C. H. MALLOCK from Command of 2 Section to Adjt. 3 D.A.C. | |
| 23.5.15 | " " E.J.B. Mackenzie " " 3 " to 42 Bde RFA | |
| 28.5.15 | Major A Murray-SMITH from 48th Div Arty to Command N°1 Section | |
| 31.5.15 | 2/Lt A IBBITSON from N°4 Sec to TRENCH N°WR Bde 2nd Army. | |
| 27.5.15 | RESPIRATORS. for use in case of 'gas' attack, issued to all ranks. | |

A J Hughes
Comdg 3 Colonel RFA
Div Ammn Col

3rd Division

3rd Div: Armour " Coy

Vol V 1 — 30.6.15

June 1915 – Sheet 1.    3rd Div Amtn Column Army Form C. 2118.

# WAR DIARY
or
# INTELLIGENCE SUMMARY.
(Erase heading not required.)

Instructions regarding War Diaries and Intelligence Summaries are contained in F.S. Regs., Part II. and the Staff Manual respectively. Title pages will be prepared in manuscript.

| Hour, Date, Place | Summary of Events and Information | Remarks and references to Appendices |
|---|---|---|
| 1st June 1915  6 am | A Detachment of 17 NCOs & men 23 horses 4 wagons 9 S with 50 rst amtn from 2nd Div Am Col Attached to No 1 Section | |
| 1st to 4th June. BELGIUM | In bivouac on WESTOUTRE - POPERINGHE Road. | |
| 4th June 9 am | H.Q 1, 2 & 3 Sections moved to position N.E of POPERINGHE Sections occupied farm lands. Officers & men bivouacked. Horses and Wagons, concealed as much as possible along hedges & under trees | |
| 5th to 11th June POPERINGHE | Normal conditions. | |
| 12th – 15th June —"— HOOGE | Supplying ammunition. 24,650 rounds of 18pr Ammunition were sent to the 3 F.A. Brigades for the attack at HOOGE on 15/16 June in addition 1,606,000 rounds of S.A.A was sent up. | |
| 17/18th June HOOGE 6 pm - 3 am | 11,600 rounds of 18pr were afterwards returned to Park A party of 90 NCos & men under 3 Officers (Capt Steward 1/Lts Bryan & Dickens) were employed clearing the Battlefield collecting wounded and burying the dead. A party of 40 NCos & men under 1/Lt Wary performed a similar duty on the nights 18/19th – One man was wounded | |
| 18/19th June HOOGE | | |
| 19th June POPERINGHE | Normal Supply and conditions resumed | |
| 0/24"—— | Normal Conditions. Very light rockets transferred to R.E Park Grenades | |

HEAD QUARTERS
4 JUL 1915
3 DIV. AMMN. COL.

June 1915 — Sheet 2                    3rd Div Ammn Column    Army Form C. 2118.

Instructions regarding War Diaries and Intelligence Summaries are contained in F.S. Regs., Part II. and the Staff Manual respectively. Title pages will be prepared in manuscript.

# WAR DIARY
or
## INTELLIGENCE SUMMARY.
(Erase heading not required.)

| Hour, Date, Place | Summary of Events and Information | Remarks and references to Appendices |
|---|---|---|
| 25th June — POPERINGHE | No 4 Section consisting of 1 Offr, 43 men, 53 horses, 9 G.S. wagons rejoined from 5th Div Ammn Col | |
| 27th June " | A party of 1 Offr (Lt Dickens) + 25 men went up to the trenches as a Bomb carrying party | |
| 28/30 " | Normal conditions Shells from an enemy long range gun passed over the Camp at different intervals during the month. No damage to troops. The town of POPERINGHE is generally the object | |
| 12 June | Changes in Officers Major N Murray Smith to 1 3rd Amm Sick 12.6.15 2/Lt N M Laurifield-Jones Joined from Base To 23rd 12.6.15 Capt R Maclean rejoined with No 4 Section | Back 12.6.15 |
| 4.6.15  12-6.15 25.6.15 | Honor. Stewart Regl Sgt Major J W Sheppard was mentioned in dispatches in Gazette of 23 June 15 | |

A. J. Hopper (Lieut) 3rd
Comdg 3 Div A.C.

2.7.15

3rd Division.

10/6/42

2nd Div: Arm'n Col'n

Vol VII

1-307.15(7)

July 1915          WAR DIARY          3rd Div Amm Col     Army Form C. 2118.
or
INTELLIGENCE SUMMARY
(Erase heading not required.)

| July 1915 Hour, Date, Place | Summary of Events and Information | Remarks and references to Appendices |
|---|---|---|
| 1st to 6th July 1915 In Bivouac POPERINGHE | In BIVOUAC on farm Lank New and E of POPERINGHE. Normal conditions | |
| 7th July | H.Q. Nos 1 & 3 Sections moved at 5.30 PM into |  |
| ABEELE | BIVOUAC 1½ Miles E of ABEELE Station |  |
| POPERINGHE | Nos 2 & 4 Sections remained near POPERINGHE and acted as advanced Sections and Supplied all Ammunition required by Brigades R.F.A. | |
| 8th to 25th POPERINGHE ABEELE | Nos 2 & 4 Sections in BIVOUAC HQ 1 & 3 Sections in BIVOUAC. | |
| 26th | Nos 2 & 4 Sections rejoined H-Qrs near ABEELE at 2PM owing to move of Division into a new area. |  |
| 15th July | The Supply of Ammunition was normal during the month except on Night of 15th – 900 rounds 15pr Shrapnel and on 30th July 1800 rounds of High |  |
| 30 of July | Explose & Shrapnel (18pr) and 468 of 4.5 Lyddite |  |

# WAR DIARY

**July 1915**    3rd Div Am Col

## INTELLIGENCE SUMMARY
*(Erase heading not required.)*

Army Form C. 2118.

| Hour, Date, Place | Summary of Events and Information | Remarks and references to Appendices |
|---|---|---|
| July 1915 | (1) RE. organization – The transport of the Column completed Re-organization of draught animals. On 22 June 1915 – 305 large mules were received to complete 1-2-13 Sections and on 22nd July M. L. received 16 Mules. The receipt of these animals allowed the release of 150 Heavy Draught Horses. (2) An increase of establishment of S.A.A. entailed the transfer of 5 Complete Turnouts which arrived from units as under 3 from 14th Bn'd Artillery 2 " 46th " " Changes in Officers Captain & Adjt C. H. Mallock promoted Major 30 Oct 14 2/Lieut AT Warry 1st W Riding promoted Lieutenant 22 May 1915. 3 Subalterns Joined and are posted to 23rd Bde QFA 24/26 July 15 2/Lt Carter ET, E L Morgan, and D E Horwood. | |
| 4/12 July 15 | | |

3rd Division

3rd Div'l. Amm'n Col'n

Vol VII

From 1 – 31. 8. 15

3rd Divisional Ammn Column

Army Form C. 2118.

# WAR DIARY
# or
# INTELLIGENCE SUMMARY.
(Erase heading not required.)

| Hour, Date, Place | Summary of Events and Information | Remarks and references to Appendices |
|---|---|---|
| August 1915 | | |
| August 1st | Still in same billets 1½ miles east of ABEELE | |
| August 9th & 10th | Supplied 1596 Rounds 18 pdr + 840 4.5 Howitzer. Otherwise the supply normal | |
| August 29th | 3 Baggage wagons, Six A.D. Horses & 8 Drivers returned & were taken on the strength of 3 Div Train. | |
| August 1st–6th | Transfers of officers | |
| | 2nd Lieut C.H. Dickens to Home Establishment | |
| | 2nd Lieut F.S. Green to 40th Bgde | |
| 24th | 2nd Lieut W. Wright from 40th Bgde to No 1 Sec | |
| | Major C. Mullyck to 108th Battery | |
| | Capt R.D. Stewart from No 2 to be Adjutant | |
| 31st | 2nd Lieut W. Wright from No 2 to No 1 Sect. | |
| | | R.S. Hughes Col |
| | | 3rd D.A.C. |

3rd Division

121/6918

3rd Div: Comm'n Ctr
Vol VIII
1-30 Sept. 15

Army Form C. 2118.

# WAR DIARY
## or
## INTELLIGENCE SUMMARY.
*(Erase heading not required.)*

| Hour, Date, Place | Summary of Events and Information | Remarks and references to Appendices |
|---|---|---|
| Sept 1 - | Still in Same Billet. | |
| 3 pm | Column moved to L.9.A.B. 1½ miles SW of POPERINGHE. Very wet day. | |
| 19.26 | Advanced expenditure of Ammn. 137,8650 SAA  302.11. 18/pr Shrap  7651. " HE | |
| | Transfers of Officers | |
| 8th Sept | Capt W. Batchelor fm 23 Bde A.C. to No.1 Sec | |
| 20th | 2 Lieut W.H Deeds fm Hants Yeomanry to No.3 Sec | |

A.J. Hughes Kish
Lieut 3 D.A.C.

D/
7308

3ᵘᵈ K/vaai

Oct. 15

Army Form C. 2118.

# WAR DIARY
## or
## INTELLIGENCE SUMMARY.
(Erase heading not required.)

Instructions regarding War Diaries and Intelligence Summaries are contained in F. S. Regs., Part II. and the Staff Manual respectively. Title pages will be prepared in manuscript.

| Hour, Date, Place | Summary of Events and Information | Remarks and references to Appendices |
|---|---|---|
| October 1st In billets 1 mile W of POPERINGHE | Still in same billets | |
| October 26th | Moved to new billets STEENVOORDE. 111 Div in rest. Transfer of officers. 2nd Lieut W. Wright to England Capt W. K. Batchelor invalided to England | |
| October 19th 23rd | | |

1-XI-15

A J Hyams Col RFA
Comdy 33 B C

Forms/C. 2118/10
(9 29 6) W 4141—463  100,000  9/14  H W V

3rd Dist Annual Conf.
No 5 / Vol X

121/7655

Army Form C. 2118.

# WAR DIARY
## or
## INTELLIGENCE SUMMARY.
(Erase heading not required.)

Instructions regarding War Diaries and Intelligence Summaries are contained in F.S. Regs., Part II. and the Staff Manual respectively. Title pages will be prepared in manuscript.

| Hour, Date, Place | Summary of Events and Information | Remarks and references to Appendices |
|---|---|---|
| Nov 1st 1915 | Still in Same billets near STEENVOORDE (At Rest) | |
| Nov 11th 11 am | Inspected by Gen Sir H. Plumer G.O.C. 2nd Army who complimented the Column on their bearing | |
| Nov 15th 10 am | Took part in Inspection of Div Arty by G.O.C. 2nd Army | |
| Nov 25th 1.30 pm | Marched from STEENVOORDE to billets near BOESCHEPE. Men in barns & tents - No horse standings | |
| | Took over from 24 DW. | |
| Nov 11th | 2 Lieut Clavey joined & posted to No.1 Sec Arty Col | Col Hughes takes Command |
| | Col Hughes took over Command Left for 2nd Army Training Camps | |
| 15th | 2 Lieut Carruthers " & posted to No.1 S.r.c. | |
| 23rd | 2 " Kidd " " 2 | |
| | 2 " Slim " " 3 | |
| 26th | 2 " Shuck " " 1 | |
| 23rd | 2 Lieut Barnels " " | |
| | Remarks Lieut Blegard to be temp Captain with effect from 23-11-15 | |

R.D. Steward Capt
Adjt 3:DAC

Forms/C. 2118/10

٢

|X|

١٢/١٧٥٧

غنذنيه منقذه عسكر عسى

**WAR DIARY**
or
**INTELLIGENCE SUMMARY.**

(Erase heading not required.)

Army Form C. 2118.

| Hour, Date, Place | Summary of Events and Information | Remarks and references to Appendices |
|---|---|---|
| Dec 1st | Still in Same Wells at BOESCHEPE | |
| 16th | During the month a large number of remounts have received from the Stationary Brigades to return to the Park. Several were found to Contain Dermatoses - Potrnip | |
| | 2 Lieut Carr } to 42 BAC | |
| | 2 Lieut Clancy } | |
| | 2 Lieut Tyrrell } to 3 DAC | |
| | 2 Lieut Buchan } | |
| 18th | 2 Lieut Buchan } to 30th Bgd. to hrkchin | |
| | Wheeler | |
| 30th | Major A.B. Mayne to temporary Command of Column. | |

R. F. Stewart Capt
A.V. 3. D.A.C.

## 3RD DIVISION
## DIVL. ARTILLERY

3RD DIVISIONAL AMMN COL.

JAN-DEC 1916.

3rd Divisional Artillery.

3RD DIVISIONAL AMMUNITION COLUMN.

JANUARY 1916.

Army Form C. 2118.

# WAR DIARY
## or
## INTELLIGENCE SUMMARY.
*(Erase heading not required.)*

Instructions regarding War Diaries and Intelligence Summaries are contained in F.S. Regs., Part II. and the Staff Manual respectively. Title pages will be prepared in manuscript.

| Hour, Date, Place | Summary of Events and Information | Remarks and references to Appendices |
|---|---|---|
| Jan 1st 1916 | Still in Same Billets at BOESCHEPE. Nothing of importance to report during the last week of the month, the Column sent up several thousand rounds of 18 p# HE in exchange for Shrapnel | |
| Jan 13th | Potinze 2 Lieut Tyacke posted to 108 Battery | |

R S-Stewart Capt.
Adj 3 BAC

3rd Divisonal Artillery.

3RD DIVISIONAL AMMUNITION COLUMN.

FEBRUARY 1916.

Army Form C. 2118.

# WAR DIARY
## or
## INTELLIGENCE SUMMARY.
*(Erase heading not required.)*

Instructions regarding War Diaries and Intelligence Summaries are contained in F. S. Regs., Part II. and the Staff Manual respectively. Title pages will be prepared in manuscript.

| Hour, Date, Place | Summary of Events and Information | Remarks and references to Appendices |
|---|---|---|
| Feb 1st | Still in Same billets in BOESCHEPE. | |
| 12th | The Column marched from BOESCHEPE to ZOUAFQUES via WEMAERS CAPPEL where it stopped the night. | |
| 13 | Arrived at ZOUAFQUES, the horse lines were found to be too exposed so were consequently moved | |
| 21 | Reduction of Establishment. | |
| 25th | 6 8 3 trains Complete & Summer 18 horses were posted to 109th Battery & particulars & WULVERDINGHE under 2 Lieut Sopran (?) to reform on Completion of duty. 1 Bomb. 1 S Smith 1 Rider jobs to 109 Batt'y. | |
| 27th | No 1. 2. & 3 Sections moved into new Billets at ARDENFORT — CAHEN & LE POIRIER respectively. | |
| 29th | Col A.T. Hughes & Secondly 2 Army Artillery Training Camp inspected the Column. | |

Forms/C. 2118/10

# WAR DIARY
## or
## INTELLIGENCE SUMMARY.
*(Erase heading not required.)*

Army Form C. 2118

| Hour, Date, Place | Summary of Events and Information | Remarks and references to Appendices |
|---|---|---|
| ZOUAFQUES 4-2-16 | Continued. Postings. | |
| | Lieut H.M. TOWNSHEND R.A.M.C. from 8th F.A.MB. 3/2/16 Vice Capt | |
| | W. RUSSELL R.A.M.C. to Royal Scots Training. | |
| 3-2-16 | 2 Lieut C.R. SHIELL to 40th Bgd. | |
| | " R.E. BENNETT to h/l Sec } from Base | |
| | " G.G. KOOP — 2 — } | |
| | " H.F.T. CLEAVER — 3 — } | |
| 6.2.16 | " E.G.S. LEADAM to Schummry from 22/2/16 from Base | |
| 16.2.16 | R.S.M. Commission 6/2/16 & posted to Base 16/2/16. | |
| 18.2.16 | B.Q.M.S. C.A. Fairburn to acting W.O. (A1) from 6/2/16 vice Abbs | |
| | 2 Lieut WHEELER rejoined to 2 Sec from Hospital. | |
| 19.2.16 | Major A.B. MAYNE to temp Lieut Col. whilst commdg Column from 17/1/16 | |
| 22.2.16 | 2 Lieut W.A.P. LANDON (SR) to h/l Sec } from BASE | |
| | A.F. LOVE " 2 . } | |
| | M.D. Williams (T.C.) " 3 . } | |
| 24-2-16 | T. DANIELS to 42 Bgd. | |
| | 96 KOOP 23 | |
| | H.F.T. CLEAVER 30 | |
| 29.2.16 | Capt J. HUGHES to command the Column. | |

R.D. Stewart Capt
A.Adj 3 DAC
1—11—15

3rd Divisional Artillery.

## 3RD DIVISIONAL AMMUNITION COLUMN.

### MARCH 1916.

Army Form C. 2118.

# WAR DIARY
## or
## INTELLIGENCE SUMMARY.
(Erase heading not required.)

Instructions regarding War Diaries and Intelligence Summaries are contained in F.S. Regs., Part II. and the Staff Manual respectively. Title pages will be prepared in manuscript.

| Hour, Date, Place | Summary of Events and Information | Remarks and references to Appendices |
|---|---|---|
| 1-III-16 ZOUAFQUES | Still in Same Billets | |
| 11-III-16 | The Column marched back to the line. Staying The night at NOORDPEENE & arrived at BOESCHEPE taking up the old Billets | |
| BOESCHEPE 26-III-16 | The adjutant was sent to 30th Bgd H.Qrs G 35 a to take charge of an Ammunition Dumps — Report & after this date the Column found nightly an officer & 20 men for Cable laying, which they dug in up to the Fire Trenches. | |
| 16-III-16 | 2 Lieut Landon & Williams attached to 40 Bde for inspection | |
| 22-III-16 | Capt GLYNN relieved Capt TOWNSHEND as M.O. | |

R B Steward Capt
A.g. 38th AC 1-IV-16

3rd Divisional Artillery.

3RD DIVISIONAL AMMUNITION COLUMN.

APRIL 1916.

Army Form C. 2118.

# WAR DIARY
## or
## INTELLIGENCE SUMMARY.
*(Erase heading not required.)*

| Hour, Date, Place | Summary of Events and Information | Remarks and references to Appendices |
|---|---|---|
| 1-4-16 BOESCHEPE | Column in Same Billets | |
| 12.4.16 | Moved to new Rest Billets in GODEWAERSVELDT. | |
| | Postings: | |
| | Lieut S. Williams from HAC to No 2 Sec | |
| | Lieut P. Woollen " " No 2 Sec. | |
| | Col A.J. HUGHES to temp Commandant 2nd Army Artillery Schools 18-4-16 | |
| | Major A.B. MAINE to temp Command of Column 19.4.16. | |

R. D. Stewart Capt
Adj 3 SAC  30-4-16

3rd Divisional Artillery.

## 3RD DIVISIONAL AMMUNITION COLUMN.

### MAY 1916.

3 Dn Am Col
Vol 16

# WAR DIARY
## INTELLIGENCE SUMMARY

Army Form C. 2118.

| Hour, Date, Place | Summary of Events and Information | Remarks and references to Appendices |
|---|---|---|
| GODEWAERSVELDT – 1-5-16 | Column moved from GODEWAERSWELDT to BERTHEN | |
| BERTHEN 9=16.5.16 | Reorganization of DAC took place – B.A.C.s being attached – HQrs at MONT ROUGE – No 1. WESTOUTRE No 2 Mont Rouge – No 3 LOCRE – not between | |
| Postwip Away 9.5.16 12.5.16 23.5.16 12.5.16 1.5.16 | LOCRE + DRANOUTRE. Col A T HUGHES resumed Command. 2 Column CAPT PARKER + CAPT MACLEAN TO Eng. Capt GLYNN to 1st Batt NORTH FUS. LIEUT INGRAM to 129 Batty – 2 LIEUT BENNETT to 30 Bge LIEUT RENDY to 42 B.G.D. WOOLEN 23 " LIEUT LEADAM " WILLIAMS 3 " " LANDON 40 – CHILVERD 30 " LOVE " WILLIAMS 3rd " | |
| Postings to DAC 20.5.16 21- 25- | 2 LIEUT GARNETT att 40 Bge DAVIDSON " 40 " TURPIN " 42 RITCHIE 23 TAYLOR 40 WHITAKER 40 REID 42 | R. S. Stewart Capt. for Col Comg 3 D A C |

3rd Divisional Artillery.

### 3RD DIVISIONAL AMMUNITION COLUMN.

### J U N E  1 9 1 6.

Army Form C. 2118.

# WAR DIARY
## or
## INTELLIGENCE SUMMARY.
(Erase heading not required.)

**3RD DAC**

| Hour, Date, Place | Summary of Events and Information | Remarks and references to Appendices |
|---|---|---|
| 1916 | | |
| June 1st GODEWAERSVELT | Column marched to CANADIAN AREA OUDERDOM | |
| June 3rd 10th | Formed a large DUMP. on OUDERDOM-VLAMERTINGHE Rd | |
| 17th | + supplied a large Quantity of Howitzer Amm | |
| 18th | Closed dump & marched to STAPLE. | |
| | Marched to REST BILLETS at SENINGHEM. | |
| POSTINGS etc | 2 Lieut G.R. Whitaker rejoined from 40th Bde — 40th Bde | |
| | 2 Lieut G.R. Wheeler — — 129th Bde | |
| | 2 Lieut F.D.O. Burnham — — 42 Bde. | |
| | 2 Lieut E. Ballard + attached to 23rd Bde | |
| | 2   "   E. Farquharson — — 23 — | |
| | 2   "   F.G. Gillham — — 42 — | |
| | 2   "   H. Spoor — | |
| Posted to 3rd DAC 8th | 29 | |

R.B. Steward Capt. for Col
Comndg 3 DAC
30-6-16

3rd Divisional Artillery.

3RD DIVL. AMMUNITION COLUMN.

J U L Y     1 9 1 6.

# WAR DIARY or INTELLIGENCE SUMMARY.

Army Form C. 2118

3rd D.A.C.

| Hour, Date, Place | Summary of Events and Information | Remarks and references to Appendices |
|---|---|---|
| SENINGHEM 1-7-16 July 2nd | Still in Rest Billets. | |
| July 3rd | Left SENINGHEM. Column entrained from STOMER WIZERNES & AUDRICQ. detrained at DOULENS, marched to bivouacs at BOURDON | |
| 4th | Marched from BOURDON 7.15pm arrived DAOURS | |
| 5th | Marched to point 6 miles W. of Bray, halting at | |
| 6th | VAUX SUR SOMME to 6 hours. Dump established near CARNOY under Lt WARRY. | |
| 7th | Moved bivouacs | |
| 8th | Opened Dump on BRAY ALBERT Rd. Moved Camp opposite DUMP. | |
| 18th July | During Month 2 L⁺ Kynch & Lodge were wounded 3 NCOs & men killed, 10 wounded. Following officers posted to D.A.C. | |
| | 2nd Lt ATERNS from hospital. T.A.HAY att. to 42 Bde. CAPT T. STEWART RAMC. L R WHEELER — posted to 40 Div Arty. 2nd AM KINGSBURY. Lt SPOOR — to D.A.C. att 40 Bde. L A STERLING F.E WARBURTON — 100 B.g.d. att 40 Bde. E L HUDSON A.H. WATKINS att 42 " A D WRIGHT C J BARTON att 42 " T.F SMITH J.R GALLWAY " att 42 Bga S AUSTIN — 12 Bty. CAPT N PERRIN RAMC away G V KYNCH " " " E FAIRBROTHER to 22nd Bga C E LANHAM att 40 Bty W BETTLES " att 41 " | |

3rd Divisional Artillery

3rd DIVISIONAL AMMUNITION COLUMN

AUGUST 1 9 1 6

Army Form C. 2118

Vol 19

# WAR DIARY
## or
## INTELLIGENCE SUMMARY.

3 D.A.C.

(Erase heading not required.)

| Hour, Date, Place | Summary of Events and Information | Remarks and references to Appendices |
|---|---|---|
| Aug 1st | In same billets ½ N of BRAY on ALBERT RD | |
| 2nd | Went into rest to Ruin ANCRE near VILLE SUR CORBIE | |
| 15th | Returned to Old billets on BRAY ALBERT RD | |
| | Reformed the DUMP. | |
| | Following officers were posted to the Column during the month. | |
| | CAPT E.J. BODY | |
| | LIEUT H.A.A. BORNE | |
| | F.E.L. PHILLIPS RAMC | |
| | 2/LIEUT B. ALDWINCKLE | |
| | ―― T.W.E. WILSON | |
| | ―― T.A.E. GREEN | |
| | ―― E.R. STAGG | |
| | ―― C.F.R. BRUCE | |
| | ―― E.F. COCHRANE | |
| | ―― W.E. RUSSELL | |
| | ―― D. SMITH | |
| | ―― G.H. STEVENS | |
| | ―― E.K. PAGE | |
| | ―― J. GORST | |

R.D. Steward Capt fr Col
Comdg 3 DAC. 31-8-16

3rd Divisional Artillery.

3RD DIVL. AMMUNITION COLUMN.

SEPTEMBER 1916.

Army Form C. 2118.

# WAR DIARY
## or
## INTELLIGENCE SUMMARY.   3 D.A.C.

*(Erase heading not required.)*

1st to 30th Sep. 1916.

WR 20

| 1916 Hour, Date, Place | Summary of Events and Information | Remarks and references to Appendices |
|---|---|---|
| Sept 1st | In Same billets on BRAY-ALBERT Rd. | |
| 7th – 13th | marched from above billets to VERQUIN | |
| | via BEHENCOURT - ORVILLE - LIGNY - BERGUENEUSE | |
| 24th | marched to THEROUANNE arriving on 25th | |
| 27 | " to WITTERNESSE | |
| | | |
| | Postings of Officers | |
| | Lieut G Ballard invalided to England | |
| | " Tebbs to hospital | |
| | 2nd Lieut A N Kingsbury ⎫ to 23rd Bgd at H Krathum | |
| |      E L Hodgson ⎬ Lieut H A A BURNE ⎫ to 42 Bgd | |
| |      L A Sterling ⎭ 2" R F Cochrane ⎬ has Posted | |
| |      F D Davidson ⎫ | |
| |      2R Shutt ⎬ | |
| |      T W Burnham ⎭ | |
| |      E K Page ⎫ to 40 Bgd | |
| |      A D Wyatt ⎬ | |
| |      C E Lanthum ⎭ | |
| |      F A Brown ⎫ to 42 Bgd | |
| |      C J Barton ⎬ | |
| |      To Allondale ⎭ | |

R.D. Plewman
Capt for Lt Col
Comdg 3 D.A.C

3rd Divisional Artillery.

### 3RD DIVL. AMMUNITION COLUMN.

### OCTOBER 1916.

Vol 21

# WAR DIARY
## or
## INTELLIGENCE SUMMARY.

3ʳᵈ D.A.C   1ˢᵗ - 31ˢᵗ Oct.

Army Form C. 2118.

(Erase heading not required.)

| Hour, Date, Place | Summary of Events and Information | Remarks and references to Appendices |
|---|---|---|
| Oct 1ˢᵗ<br>Still at Château La Tournière<br>Oct 5 | Marched to VARENNES, staying the night of 5ᵗʰ at BERGUENEUSE AREA & TILLY CAPELLE & the 6ᵗʰ at ETREE WAMIN. | |
| 8. | Took over ARP at ACHEUX - BERTRANCOURT Rᴅ from 2ⁿᵈ Div. | |
| 17. | Moved 'A' Echelon near ARP, 'B' Echelon to SARTON | |
| | POSTINGS of OFFICERS | |
| | Lieut WHO'KEEFE from Base 22-10-16 att 40ᵗʰ Bgd. | |
| | 2ᴸⁱᵉᵘᵗ G.W.G. BAASS  " " " " att 40ᵗʰ Bgd. | |
| | 2ᴸᵗ DNK BAIRD  " " " " | |
| | " WWB FAUSSET  " " " " att 40 Bgd. | |
| | " J.R. TATEM  " " " " | |

W.J. Murphy<br>Col RFA<br>Comdg 3 DAC<br>31-10-16

3rd Divisional Artillery.

3RD DIVL. AMMUNITION COLUMN.

NOVEMBER 1916.

1st to 30th Nov, 1916

Army Form C. 2118

# WAR DIARY
## or
## INTELLIGENCE SUMMARY.
(Erase heading not required.)

3 DAC

| Hour, Date, Place | Summary of Events and Information | Remarks and references to Appendices |
|---|---|---|
| Nov 1st | Still at SARTON ACHEUX | |
| 4. | HdQrs + A Echelon moved to ~~ACHEUX~~ SARTON | |
| 11 | A Echelon moved back to ACHEUX. | |
| 12. | Hd Qrs    "     "      "      " | |
| 20 | A Echelon moved to SARTON from | |
|  | B Echelon left SARTON, moved to ACHEUX. | |

R L Stewart Cpl
Any 3 DAC

1/12/16

Forms/C. 2118/10

3rd Divisional Artillery.

3RD DIVL. AMMUNITION COLUMN.

DECEMBER 1916.

Army Form C. 2118

Vol 23

# WAR DIARY
## or
## INTELLIGENCE SUMMARY.
*(Erase heading not required.)*

3 D.A.C.
1st to 31st Dec 1916

| Hour, Date, Place | Summary of Events and Information | Remarks and references to Appendices |
|---|---|---|
| Dec 1st 7" 15" 16 | Still at ACHEUX. Hd Qrs moved to ORVILLE No 2 Sec went to AUTHIE WOOD returned to ORVILLE | |

R. S. Steward Capt.
Adj 3 D.A.C.

2nd Division
War Diaries

D. A. C.

January to December
1917

1st to 31st Jan. 1914.

Army Form C. 2118.

3 D.A.C.

3 Vol 24

# WAR DIARY
## or
## INTELLIGENCE SUMMARY.
(Erase heading not required.)

| Hour, Date, Place | Summary of Events and Information | Remarks and references to Appendices |
|---|---|---|
| Jan 1st | "B" echelon still at Acheux. HQ. 2 + 3 Secs still at Orville. 1 Sec at Authie Wood | |
| 15th | HQ. 2 + 3 Secs marched to St Ouen via Authie Wood | |
| 16th | 1 Sec + "B" echelon marched to St Ouen via Doullens, Candas, Fieffes, Canaples, Bertrancourt. | |
| 22nd | D.A.C. billeted in St Ouen. 2 Officers + 72 ORs joined from 31st D.A. to form 23 B.A.C. | |
| 23rd | Reorganization of D.A.C. no 3 Sec with additional from 131st D.A. becomes 23rd Bde: Am: Col: with Lt A.T. WARRY in command. | Acting / am of adj 3 D.A.C. |
| 29th | D.A.C. marched to Authieule via Canaples, Candas. Billets for the night. | |
| 30th | March continued to Conchy via Doullens, Frévent. Billets here until Feb 1st when march was continued | |

Feb. 1st to 26th. 1917

Army Form C. 2118.

3 DAC

# WAR DIARY
## or
## INTELLIGENCE SUMMARY.
(Erase heading not required.)

Instructions regarding War Diaries and Intelligence Summaries are contained in F.S. Regs., Part II. and the Staff Manual respectively. Title pages will be prepared in manuscript.

| Hour, Date, Place | Summary of Events and Information | Remarks and references to Appendices |
|---|---|---|
| Feb 1st | Column continued march to BAJUS via FRÉVENT TERNAS BAILLEUL. The frozen condition of the roads made travelling exceedingly difficult. | |
| 5th | "B" echelon moved to WANQUETIN to relieve the 35th "B" echelon on Engineering work | |
| 8th | Transferred from XVII Corps to VI + moved to WAMIN via MAGNICOURT, BAILLEUL, MAZIERES. | |
| 19th | A.R.P. formed at WANQUETIN | |
| 21st to 26th | "B" echelon moved to HAUTEVILLE | |

A.C. Kingham 2/Lt R.F.A.
a/adj 3DAC.

(2 29 6) W 4141—463 100,000 9/14 H W V Forms/C. 2118/10

Army Form C. 2118.

# WAR DIARY
## or
## INTELLIGENCE SUMMARY.
(Erase heading not required.)

1st to 31 March 1917

3 D A C

| Hour, Date, Place | Summary of Events and Information | Remarks and references to Appendices |
|---|---|---|
| | | Ref. 1:40,000 Sheet 51.C |
| March 1st | A echelon still at WAMIN. B echelon at HAUTEVILLE. | |
| 2nd | H.Q. + 1 Section moved to WANQUITIN via AVESNES-LA-COMTE. 2 Section moved to HAUTEVILLE. Still billeted. | |

W Kingham Lt
aaj 3DAC

1st to 30 April 17

Army Form C. 2118.

# WAR DIARY
## or
## INTELLIGENCE SUMMARY.

(Erase heading not required.)

3 D.A.C.

Instructions regarding War Diaries and Intelligence Summaries are contained in F.S. Regs., Part II. and the Staff Manual respectively. Title pages will be prepared in manuscript.

| Hour, Date, Place | Summary of Events and Information | Remarks and references to Appendices |
|---|---|---|
| 1917 April 1st | Still at WANQUETIN. | |
| 8th | No 1 S.C. moved up to RACECOURSE ARRAS | |
| 10th | No 2 S.C. + Kemainder of no 1 ditto | |
| 9th | A.R.P. Commenced to move from WARLUS to QUAI des CASERNES | |
| 11th | H.Q. + No 3 Moved up to RACE COURSE ARRAS | |
| 13th | Commenced dumping at ALBEANEY CAVE. | |
| 27th | Formed new A.R.P. at TILLOY M.6.B.5.6. (Sheet 51B) | |
| | for 4L Bgde + ALBEANEY CAVE being transferred to 4th D.A.C. | |

15/17

R. D. Steward Capt fr Col
Cmdg 3 DAC

Forms/C. 2118/10

1st to 31st May 1917.

Army Form C. 2118.

# WAR DIARY
## INTELLIGENCE SUMMARY.
*(Erase heading not required.)*

3RD D.A.C.

Instructions regarding War Diaries and Intelligence Summaries are contained in F.S. Regs., Part II. and the Staff Manual respectively. Title pages will be prepared in manuscript.

| Hour, Date, Place | Summary of Events and Information | Remarks and references to Appendices |
|---|---|---|
| 1917 | | |
| May 1st. | H.Q. and Nos. 2 & 3 Sections still at ARRAS. No. 1 Section still at TILLOY. | |
| May 15th. | A.R.P. at ALDERNEY CAVE finally closed, and ammunition transferred to existing A.R.P. at TILLOY. | |
| May 28th. | "A" Echelon Sections ceased to be attached to 40th. and 42nd. Bdes. H.Q., No. 2 Section and "B" Echelon moved from RACECOURSE to a point about 300 yds. NORTH of ARRAS – DAINVILLE ROAD. | |
| May 29th. | No. 1 Section moved from TILLOY and camped with the rest of the D.A.C. Aire Balfour alt. for Col. Grundy, 3 D.A.C. | |

1st to 30th June 1917.

Army Form C. 2118.

# WAR DIARY
## or
## INTELLIGENCE SUMMARY
(Erase heading not required.)

3RD D A C

Vol 29

| Place | Date | Hour | Summary of Events and Information | Remarks and references to Appendices |
|---|---|---|---|---|
| ARRAS | 1.6.17 | | D.A.C. still in bivouacs in field 300 yds N of ARRAS DAINVILLE Rd. G.20.0.12 Sheet 51B. | |
| TILLOY | 22.6.17 | | A.R.P. closed | |
| ACHICOURT | " | | Took over 29th Div. A.R.P. | |
| " | 23.6.17 | | Handed over A.R.P. to 61st Div. | |
| ARRAS | 24.6.17 | | D.A.C. moved to SIMENCOURT and BERNEVILLE & look at fields | |

J. D. C.
Lt Col RFA
Comdg 3rd DAC

Army Form C. 2118.

3RD D.A.C.

1st – 31st JULY '17

## WAR DIARY
## or
## INTELLIGENCE SUMMARY.
(Erase heading not required.)

| Place | Date | Hour | Summary of Events and Information | Remarks and references to Appendices |
|---|---|---|---|---|
| SIMENCOURT | July 1st | | D.A.C. left SIMENCOURT and marched to BAPAUME via BEAUMETZ - RIVIERE - RANSART - ADINFER - ABLAINZEVELLE - ACHIET-LE-GRAND - BIHUCOURT and bivouaced at H28a (Sheet 57c) just EAST of BAPAUME. | |
| BAPAUME | July 7th | | 'A' Echelon marched to MILL CROSS (I 27c - Sheet 57c):- 'B' Echelon marched to near HAPLINCOURT (O2d - Sheet 57c) - and bivouaced | |
| | July 7th | | TOOK over A.R.P. at I 21d - Sheet 57c. from 1st AUSTRALIAN D.A.C. | |

G.S. Eadam
2/Lt RPA
for Adj. 3rd D.A.C.

Army Form C. 2118.

# WAR DIARY
## or
## INTELLIGENCE SUMMARY.
(Erase heading not required.)

3rd D.A.C.
From 1st to 31st August (Milburn)

WO 31

| Place | Date | Hour | Summary of Events and Information | Remarks and references to Appendices |
|---|---|---|---|---|
| | Aug 1st to Aug 31st | | D.A.C. entrained - Nos 1 & 2 Sections at MILL CROSS (Sheet 57c I27c) No 3 Section near HAPLINCOURT (Sheet 57c O2d) | |
| | Aug 31st | | The completion of re-organization of D.A.C. under G.H.Q. Letter No O.B./2038 dated 19th July, 1917, under which the Composition of D.A.C. is :- A Headquarters. 2 Sections - Each equivalent to an Army F.A. Artillery Bde Ammunition Column - and carrying Gun - ammunition only; 1 S.A.A Section to S.A.A Reserve only. | |

C Adams
L.C. Adams
Lt RNA
for Adjutant 3rd D.A.C.

Army Form C. 2118.

From 1st to 30th September 1917.

3 D.A.C.

Vol 32

# WAR DIARY
# INTELLIGENCE SUMMARY.
(Erase heading not required.)

| Place | Date | Hour | Summary of Events and Information | Remarks and references to Appendices |
|---|---|---|---|---|
| MILL CROSS | Sept 1st | | D.A.C. remained. H.Q's, Nos 1 & 2 SECTIONS at MILL CROSS (Sheet 57c. I27c.) No 3 Section near HAPLINCOURT (Sheet 57c O2 d). | |
| | Sept 15th | | D.A.C. Entrained at BAPAUME WEST and proceeds via ARRAS to PROVEN, detraining on the 16th Sept and marched to WATOU where the D.A.C. Encamped. | |
| | Sept 23rd | | No 3 Section 3rd D.A.C. moved to a Camp 1½ miles EAST of BOESINGHE on the POPERINGHE – VLAMERTINGHE Rd at G10a 5.5. (Sheet 28). | |
| | Sept 27th | | 3rd D.A.C. took over Dumps from 9th D.A.C. —<br>VANCOUVER DUMP H14.6.4.8.<br>MOAT " H17.C.7.4. } Sheet 28.<br>"A" " H12.6.5.6.<br>"B" (MILL COTE) " C.29.c.5.1. | |
| | Sept 27th<br>Sept 29th | | H.Q. 3rd D.A.C. moved to G.10.6.5.5 (Sheet 28) EAST of POPERINGHE. Nos 1 and 2 Section moved to a Camp 1½ miles EAST of POPERINGHE on the POPERINGHE – VLAMERTINGHE Rd G.10.a. (Sheet 28). | |

G.S. Badans
Major 3rd D.A.C.

Army Form C. 2118.

# WAR DIARY
## or
## INTELLIGENCE SUMMARY.
(Erase heading not required.)

**3DAC** 1st – 31st October 1917

| Place | Date | Hour | Summary of Events and Information | Remarks and references to Appendices |
|---|---|---|---|---|
| G10 b Sheet 28 | 1/10/17 | | The Column was engaged at this point "packing" Ammunition to batteries | |
| | 17/10/17 | | marched to WINNEZEELE on being relieved by the 3rd Canadian DAC who took over Dumps & Camps. | |
| | 19/10/17 | | marched to EECKE AREA. | |
| | 22/10/17 | | Entrained to BAPAUME + | |
| | 24/10/17 | | Marched to GOMIECOURT | |
| | 27/10/17 | | Took over Camp from 62 DAC at H2b Sheet 57c on the BAPAUME – BEUGNATRE Rd. | |

R. D. Stewart Capt
Comdg 3DAC
31/10/17

Army Form C. 2118.

3 BTAC from 1st to 30th November 1917

WAR DIARY
or
INTELLIGENCE SUMMARY.
(Erase heading not required.)

| Place | Date | Hour | Summary of Events and Information | Remarks and references to Appendices |
|---|---|---|---|---|
| BAPAUME | 30-11-17 | | In Same Willets | |

30/11/17  R. Steward Capt
          Adj 3 BTAC

Army Form C. 2118.

# WAR DIARY
## or
## INTELLIGENCE SUMMARY.
(Erase heading not required.)

3 D.A.C.

Instructions regarding War Diaries and Intelligence Summaries are contained in F.S. Regs., Part II. and the Staff Manual respectively. Title pages will be prepared in manuscript.

| Place | Date | Hour | Summary of Events and Information | Remarks and references to Appendices |
|---|---|---|---|---|
| | 12-11-17 | 12 noon | HARROGATE Group T.1 & 4 South of VAULX VAUCOURT handed over to 25th Division. | 41 36 |
| | 15/11/17 | 9 am | Column marched to new camp North of GOMIECOURT No 1 and 2 section A 16 d 5.8 for: and S.A.A. Section A 24 a 0.2 | |
| | 31/12 | | entire personnel 87 other ranks joined | |
| | 24/12 | | | |

31/12/17.

W J Hughes Lieut
2nd/3 DAC

**3RD DIVISION**
**DIVL. ARTILLERY**

3RD DIVL. AMMN COLUMN.
1918

Army Form C. 2118.

3rd. D.A.C.
From 1st to 31st January 1918

# WAR DIARY
or
# INTELLIGENCE SUMMARY.
(Erase heading not required.)

Instructions regarding War Diaries and Intelligence Summaries are contained in F.S. Regs., Part II. and the Staff Manual respectively. Title pages will be prepared in manuscript.

| Place | Date | Hour | Summary of Events and Information | Remarks and references to Appendices |
|---|---|---|---|---|
| GOMIÉCOURT | 31·1·18. | | In same billets. | |

J.S. Rasburn Major
OC of 3rd D.A.C.

Army Form C. 2118.

3rd. Div. Am. Col.
From 1st to 28th February 1918.

Vol 37

# WAR DIARY
or
## INTELLIGENCE SUMMARY.
(Erase heading not required.)

Instructions regarding War Diaries and Intelligence Summaries are contained in F.S. Regs., Part II. and the Staff Manual respectively. Title pages will be prepared in manuscript.

| Place | Date | Hour | Summary of Events and Information | Remarks and references to Appendices |
|---|---|---|---|---|
| GOMIECOURT | 1-2-18 | — | In same billets. | |
| HENU | 11-2-18 | | The 3rd D.A.C. marched to HENU AREA. HQ and No.1 SECTION HENU No. 2 " No. 3 " GAUDIEMPRE. | |
| HENU | 13-2-18 | | The 3rd D.A.C. in same area. | |

E. Fagan Major
Offg 3rd D.A.C.

3rd Divisional Artillery.

3rd DIVISIONAL AMMUNITION COLUMN R.F.A.

MARCH 1918

Army Form C. 2118.

3 D Amm Col
Vol 38

# WAR DIARY
or
# INTELLIGENCE SUMMARY.
(Erase heading not required.)

Instructions regarding War Diaries and Intelligence Summaries are contained in F.S. Regs., Part II. and the Staff Manual respectively. Title pages will be prepared in manuscript.

| Place | Date | Hour | Summary of Events and Information | Remarks and references to Appendices |
|---|---|---|---|---|
| HENU | March 1st | — | H.Q. and No 1 Section 3rd D.A.C. at HENU. Sheet 57 D. C 24 6. | |
| GAUDIEMPRE | " " | — | No 2 and No 3 " 3rd D.A.C. at GAUDIEMPRE Sheet 51 B. Y 25 d | |
| HENDECOURT | " 2nd | 9 a.m. | The 3rd D.A.C. marched from HENU and GAUDIEMPRE to FICHEUX. Wagon lines and Encamped. Map Ref. Sheet 51 B. S 7 d and S 7 b. | |
| " | " 3rd | — | The 3rd D.A.C. took over A.R.P. at MERCATEL. Sheet 51 B. M 23 d. | |
| " | " " | — | The 3rd D.A.C. supplied working party to dig reserve gun positions behind the front covered by 3rd D.A. looking back. Encamped at M 36 d Sheet 51 B. | |
| " | Mond 22/23 Midnight | — | The S.A.A. Section 3rd D.A.C. delivered at NEUVILLE VITASSE - the whole of their establishment of S.A.A. at N 21 a 8.9. (Sheet 51B) and at N 26 c.1.8. (Sheet 51B). | |
| BRETENCOURT | " 24th | 9.30 a.m | The 3rd D.A.C. marched forward S BRETENCOURT and Encamped at BLAIREVILLE - BRETENCOURT Rd at R 34 a and R 27 d.: (Sheet 51 c.). The 3rd D.A.C. took over ½ of A.R.P. on BLAIREVILLE - BRETENCOURT Rd. Guards Divn. Ro Rova. the other ½ of A.R.D. | |
| " | " " | " | The A.R.D. at MERCATEL Sheet 51B M 23 d. closed and evacuated. | |
| " | " 26 | 12 noon | The S.A.A. Sectn. 3rd D.A.C. dumped 1000 Boxes of S.A.A. along the Purple Line. | |

Army Form C. 2118.

# WAR DIARY
## or
## INTELLIGENCE SUMMARY.
*(Erase heading not required.)*

Instructions regarding War Diaries and Intelligence Summaries are contained in F. S. Regs., Part II. and the Staff Manual respectively. Title pages will be prepared in manuscript.

| Place | Date | Hour | Summary of Events and Information | Remarks and references to Appendices |
|---|---|---|---|---|
| | March | | | |
| BRETENCOURT | 28th | – | A.R.D. on BLAIREVILLE – BRETENCOURT Issued 30,000 15bdr – and 5000 4.5" | |
| " | 29th | 12 noon | The S.a.a. Section 3rd D.A.C. Continued to deliver S.A.R. | |
| " | 30th | 12 noon | The 1st Canadian N.A.C. took over A.R.D. from 3rd D.A.C. | |
| | | 6 pm | The " " " relieved 3rd D.A.C. | |
| BAVINCOURT | " | 2pm | The S.A.A. Section 3rd D.A.C. marched to BAVINCOURT. | |
| | | 6pm | The H.Q. No.1 and No.2 Section of 3rd D.A.C. marched to BAVINCOURT. | |
| BAVINCOURT | 31st | – | The 3rd D.A.C. remained at BAVINCOURT. | |

3rd Divisional Artillery

WAR DIARY

3rd DIVISIONAL AMMUNITION COLUMN

APRIL 1918

Army Form C. 2118.

# WAR DIARY
## or
## INTELLIGENCE SUMMARY.
(Erase heading not required.)

3 D.A.C.
From 1st to 30th April 1918

| Place | Date | Hour | Summary of Events and Information | Remarks and references to Appendices |
|---|---|---|---|---|
| BAVINCOURT | APRIL 1 | | The Column marched from BAVINCOURT to RAMICOURT (S1 st 63) | |
| | 2 | | — — RAMICOURT to AHETTES (D 34 42) | |
| | 4 | | — — AHETTES to RAIMBERT (C 10 L53) | |
| | 9 | | No 1 Sec — RAIMBERT to BETHUNE (To Inf) | |
| | 9 | | Nos No 2 + 3 Secs — LAPUGNOY (B 10 b 32) | |
| | 10 | | No 1 Sec marched from BETHUNE to L'ABBE CABOOLES (W 25 06) | |
| | 10 | | No 1 Sec " " CHOQUES to VENDIN-LES-BETHUNE (W 36 L3w) | |
| | 11 | | No 1 Sec " " VENDIN to LAPUGNOY (D 16 c 58) | |
| | 12 | | No 1 Sec " " LAPUGNOY to OBLINGHEM (form) | |
| | 12 | | No 3 Sec " " OBLINGHEM to LAPUGNOY (D 17 c 4 2) | |
| | 13 | | " " Closed OBLINGHEM dump + opened at LAPUGNOY | |
| | 14 | | No 1 Sec Started ARP at VENDIN to 4 2 Bgn | |
| | 15 | | No 2 Sec " " LABEUVRIERE to 4 9 1 gn | |

1/5/18

Capt.
Comm'g 3 A.C.

Army Form C. 2118.

# WAR DIARY
## or
## INTELLIGENCE SUMMARY.
(Erase heading not required.)

3 D A C
From 1st to 31st May 1916

WO 40

| Place | Date | Hour | Summary of Events and Information | Remarks and references to Appendices |
|---|---|---|---|---|
| LAPUGNOY | MAY 1st 1916 | — | HQ. } 3RD DAC. <br> No 1 SECTION <br> No 2 <br> S.A.A. | |
| | 13th Mon 15th Wed | — | No 1 Section 3rd D.A.C. marched from LAPUGNOY to D8c7.2. (Sheet 36B) 11/5/16. <br> HQ 3rd DAC marched from LAPUGNOY to D7c8.3 (Sheet 36B) 15/5/16. <br> No 2 Section - 3rd DAC " " to D15b.4.4. (Sheet 36B) 13/5/16 <br> F.A.A Section 3rd DAC " " to D4a.9.7. (Sheet 36B) 13/5/16. | |
| | 14th Mon 16th Mon 13th | | S.A.A. Dump moved from ANNEZIN. L9a to D11d5.2. (BETHUNE - Embrad Rd). <br> In I see two horse lines were shelled. One shell killing 38 + wounding <br> 39 animals. 23 of which were sent to X1 Mobile Section. | |
| | 16 | | S.A.A. Section formed 2 S.A.A. Reserve dumps at D24d3.7. and D2c5.6. | |

RH Stewart Capt
a/y 3rd AC

1/6/18

Army Form C. 2118.

From 1st June to 30th June 1918

3rd D.A.C.

Vol 41

# WAR DIARY
or
# INTELLIGENCE SUMMARY.
(Erase heading not required.)

Instructions regarding War Diaries and Intelligence Summaries are contained in F. S. Regs., Part II. and the Staff Manual respectively. Title pages will be prepared in manuscript.

| Place | Date | Hour | Summary of Events and Information | Remarks and references to Appendices |
|---|---|---|---|---|
| June | 1st | | Here to 2nd Batteries in Same Camps D.8.d.2.3 + D.14.a.9.9 + D.8.d.7.8 — See Maps to D.8.d.7.8 — | |
| | 10th | | New A.R.P. Commenced at REST STATION LABEUVRIERE | |
| | 29th | | Reduced Establishment of the Column came into force | |

R. D. Stewart Capt
Adj 3 DAC

Army Form C. 2118.

# WAR DIARY
## or
## INTELLIGENCE SUMMARY.
(Erase heading not required.)

3rd D.A.C. From 1st to 31st July 1918

| Place | Date | Hour | Summary of Events and Information | Remarks and references to Appendices |
|---|---|---|---|---|
| D8d2.3. (Bezuve enfants sheet) | 1/7/18 | — | Reduction of Establishment by 36 Drivers and 72 L.D.H. in accordance with Amendment to War Establishment No 818 dated June 1918. | Vol 4 |

A.S. Instance
for Capt. Comdg. 3rd D.A.C.

Army Form C. 2118.

From 1st to 31st August 1918

# WAR DIARY
or
## INTELLIGENCE SUMMARY.
(Erase heading not required.)

3rd D.A.C.                  Sheet 1.

Instructions regarding War Diaries and Intelligence Summaries are contained in F.S. Regs. Part II. and the Staff Manual respectively. Title pages will be prepared in manuscript.

| Place | Date AUG | Hour | Summary of Events and Information | Remarks and references to Appendices |
|---|---|---|---|---|
| D8d.2.3. | 1/8/18 | - | No 2 Section moved from D14.a.9.9. to I6a.8.3. (Sheet 44B) | |
| B8c.4.7. | 7/8/18 | - | HQ. No 1 and No 3 Section marched from D8d.2.3. to NEDON B8c.4.7. (Sheet 44B) | |
| NEDON. | 13/8/18 | 10pm | Marched from NEDON - arrived CANETTEMONT 9am 14th with trouble. H25a.2.9. (Sheet 51c) | |
| CANETTEMONT | 14/8/18 | - | No 2 Section marched from I6a.8.3. (Sheet 44B) to CANETTEMONT. Moved from CANETTEMONT to HUMBERCOURT O13c.8.0. (Sheet 51c) | |
| HUMBERCOURT | 20/8/18 | - | Marched from HUMBERCOURT to HUMBERCAMP. V.29.a.5.3. (Sheet 51c) | |
| " | 21/8/18 | - | Took over WHIZZ DUMP. and BANG DUMP. | |
| " | 22/8/18 | - | DUMP starts at W.29.c. (Sheet 51c) 22/8/18. S.A.A. Dump started at S.26.c.7.4. (Sheet 51c) | |
| " | 23/8/18 | - | Handed over WHIZZ & BANG DUMPS. and DUMP at W.29.c. to 2nd Div. | |
| POMMIER | 25/8/18 | - | Marched from HUMBERCAMP to POMMIER W.26.6.5. (BUCQUOY Communal Road) | |
| ADINFER WOOD | 28/8/18 | - | HQ. No 1 and No 2 Sections marched from POMMIER to ADINFER WOOD. F.3.c.5.4. (Sheet 57B) | |
| " | 29/8/18 | - | S.A.A. Section marches from POMMIER to X.22.d.1.8. (Sheet 57c). | |

R.S. Stewart Capt & Col
Commdg 3 DAC

3rd Divisional Ammunition Column
from 1st to 30th September 1918 (inclusive)

Army Form C. 2118.

# WAR DIARY
## or
## INTELLIGENCE SUMMARY.
(Erase heading not required.)

3rd D.A.C

918 44

| Place | Date | Hour | Summary of Events and Information | Remarks and references to Appendices |
|---|---|---|---|---|
| ADINFER WOOD | Sept 1st 1918 | | H.Q. - N°1 and N°2 Sections 3rd D.A.C. S.A.A. Section near BOIRY St RICTRUDE. | |
| BOIRY St RICTRUDE | 1/9/18 | | H.Q. moved to BOIRY St RICTRUDE N°1 Section to HAPLINCOURT. | |
| | 2/9/18 | | N°2 " moved to near MOYENVILLE. | |
| MORY | 6/9/18 | | H.Q. N°1 and N°2 Sections marched to an area ½ mile North of MORY | |
| ADINFER | 9/9/18 | | H.Q. N°1 and N°2 Sections " " between ADINFER and BOIRY St RICTRUDE. | |
| VAULX | 9/9/18 | | H.Q. N°1 and N°2 Sections marched to an area between VAULX - VRAUCOURT and BEUGNY - Ammunition dump at VELU Station | |
| | 11/9/18 | | S.A.A. Section marched from area of ADINFER to GOMIECOURT. | |
| | 15/9/18 | | S.A.A. Section marched from GOMIECOURT to an area between VAULX-VRAUCOURT & MORCHIES. S.A.A. dump at LEBUCQUIERE. | |
| | 16/9/18 | | N°2 Section marched from area near VAULX-VRAUCOURT to an area between BEUGNY - HAPLINCOURT. | |
| | 19/9/18 | | H.Q. moved to an area between VAULX - VRAUCOURT and MORCHIES. | |
| VELU | 27/9/18 | | H.Q. N°1 & N°2 Section marched to an area Scripts I of VELU wood and Gme with the orders | |

PAGE 2

Army Form C. 2118.

# WAR DIARY
## or
## INTELLIGENCE SUMMARY.   3rd D.A.C.

(Erase heading not required.)

| Place | Date | Hour | Summary of Events and Information | Remarks and references to Appendices |
|---|---|---|---|---|
| VELU | 27/9/18 | | of 62nd D.A. Group formed at Bgd. between ROYAULCOURT — METZ EN - COUTURE. | |
| HAVRINCOURT WOOD. | 29/9/18 | | HQ, No. 1 - 2. and J.A.A. Sectn marched to P.17. West side of HAVRINCOURT Wood. Dump formed in Q.2. HAVRINCOURT WOOD. | |
| HAVRINCOURT | 30/9/18 | | HQ. No 1 and 2 Sectn marched to HAVRINCOURT. Dump formed at RIER COURT. 3rd D.A.C took over from 62nd D.A.C at midnight on 30th Sept. | |

E.S.Hedany
M.C. O/C 3/8 D.A.C.

# WAR DIARY

## INTELLIGENCE SUMMARY

3rd D.A.C. Vol 45

| Place | Date Oct | Hour | Summary of Events and Information | Remarks and references to Appendices |
|---|---|---|---|---|
| HAVRINCOURT | 1st | - | 3rd D.A.C. HAVRINCOURT. A.R.P. at RUYAULCOURT and RIBECOURT. | |
| RIBECOURT | 2nd | - | H.Q. No1 and No2 Sections marched from HAVRINCOURT to RIBECOURT. | |
| " | 3rd | - | S.A.A. Section marched from RUYAULCOURT to HAVRINCOURT. | |
| MARCOING | 7th | - | A.R.P. established between MARCOING and MASNIERES. | |
| MARCOING | 10th | - | H.Q. No2 and SAA SECTION marched to MARCOING | |
| " | 11th | - | No1 Section marched to MARCOING. | |
| BOISTRAN- COURT | 17th | - | H.Q. No1 and 2 Section marched to BOISTRANCOURT. ½ mile South of Sugar FACTORY on CAMBRAI LE CATEAU Rd. A.R.P. at same place. | |
| " | 18th | - | No1 and 2 Sections placed 200 rounds. 18 pdr and 200. 4.5" per gun on Bty Positions 2 miles S.E. of SOLESMES. A.R.P. formed 400 yds East of QUIEVY on QUIEVY – SOLESMES Rd. | |
| QUIEVY | 23rd | - | H.Q. No1 and 2 Sections. SAA. marched to QUIEVY. Billets in EAST SIDE. Dump formed 1 mile West of SOLESMES on QUIEVY SOLESMES Rd. | |
| ROMERIES | 24th | - | H.Q. No1 and 2 and SAA SECTIONS marched to ROMERIES and Camps ¼ mile West of ROMERIES – A.R.P. formed by this Camp – and another A.R.P. ½ mile E. of ROMERIES – on ROMERIES – BEAUDIGNIES Rd. | |
| " | 26th | - | A.R.P. formed ½ mile N. of PONT DE BOIST. N.E. of CAPELLE. | |

Lt Col J Leonard
Comdg 3rd DAC

# WAR DIARY or INTELLIGENCE SUMMARY.

Army Form C. 2118.

**3rd D.A.C.** 1st – 30 Nov 1918

| Place | Date | Hour | Summary of Events and Information | Remarks and references to Appendices |
|---|---|---|---|---|
| | 1-11-18 | | Still at ROMERIES | |
| | 4-11-18 | | Move to R.31 | |
| | 5-11-18 | | Move to ORCHARD on west edge of FRESNOY, where A.R.P. was started – at 2.30 hours were shelled out; had 2 horses killed & 6 wounded | |
| | 6-11-18 | | Shifted Camp 500 yds west | |
| | 8-11-18 | | Marched to CHEVAL-BLANC | |
| | 11-11-18 | | Armistice Signed | |
| | 20-11-18 | | The Column marched to VIEUX-MESNIL | |
| | 21-11-18 | | " " ROUSIES | |
| | 25-11-18 | | " " SFLE-SUR-SAMBRE | |
| | 26-11-18 | | " " MARBAIX | |
| | 28-11-18 | | " " BIESME | |
| | 29-11-18 | | " " St GERARD | |
| | 30-11-18 | | " " YVOIR | |

William Cocker(?) Capt
Comdg 3rd DAC

Army Form C. 2118.

1st to 31st December 1918.

# WAR DIARY  3rd D.A.C.
## or
## INTELLIGENCE SUMMARY.
(Erase heading not required.)

| Place | Date | Hour | Summary of Events and Information | Remarks and references to Appendices |
|---|---|---|---|---|
| NOIR | 4.12.18 | | H.Q. No 2 and No 3 Sections marched from NOIR to DURNAL | |
| PESSOUX } TRISOGNE | 5.12.18 | | No 1 Section to CRUPET | |
| | | | The 3rd D.A.C. continued their march to PESSOUX & TRISOGNE. | |
| BAILONVILLE | 6.12.18 | | " " " " " BAILONVILLE | |
| FRONVILLE MONVILLE | 7.12.18 | | " " " " " FRONVILLE & MONVILLE | |
| FISENNE | 9.12.18 | | " " " " " FISENNE | |
| ODRIGNE | 11.12.18 | | " " " " " ODRIGNE | |
| PROVEDROUX | 12.12.18 | | " " " " " PROVEDROUX | |
| BEHO | 13.12.18 | | " " " " " BEHO | |
| THOMMEN | 14.12.18 | | " " " " " THOMMEN | |
| SCHOMBERG | 15.12.18 | | " " " " " SCHOMBERG | |
| KRONENBURGH | 16.12.18 | | " " " " " KRONENBURGH. | |
| BLANKENHEIM | 17.12.18 | | " " " " " BLANKENHEIM | |
| MECHERNICH | 18.12.18 | | " " " " " MECHERNICH | |
| WOLLERSHEIM | 19.12.18 | | " " " " " WOLLERSHEIM | |
| LENDERSDORF | 20.12.18 to 31.12.18 | | " " " " " LENDERSDORF | |

G. Pheasant
Major (aug) 3rd D.A.C.
1.1.19

~~2 ARMY TROOPS~~

3 DIV

40

TRENCH MORTAR BTY

1915 JULY TO 1916 JAN

1073

… Army Form C. 2118

## WAR DIARY
## or
## INTELLIGENCE SUMMARY
(Erase heading not required.)

II  40 [Howitzer] Bde ?

| Place | Date | Hour | Summary of Events and Information | Remarks and references to Appendices |
|---|---|---|---|---|
| 42 Bde<br>Amm. Col<br>G.10.d.3.3. | 25th<br>Aug<br>1915 | 10 p.m. | In reference to instructions received from the C.R.A., 3rd Division I arrived at BERTHEN yesterday and to-day took over command of the 40 French Howitzer Battery. I at once proceeded under the same instructions with the battery to the sidings of the 42nd Bde. Ammunition Column. A.B.<br>Lt. O.C. 40 T.H.B.<br><br>Reference:<br>BELGIUM ("B" Series) Sheet 28 N.W. | |

# WAR DIARY
## or
## INTELLIGENCE SUMMARY

Army Form C. 2118

| Place | Date | Hour | Summary of Events and Information | Remarks and references to Appendices |
|---|---|---|---|---|
| ~~4th~~ ~~Verbranden~~ ~~molen~~ Staff Horses (I 34a.6.6.) near VERBRANDEN-MOLEN South of YPRES | 28 July 1915 | 10 p.m. | In obedience to instructions received from the C.R.A., 3rd Division, last night I brought the 40th Trench Howitzer Battery up to the trenches south of YPRES. This morning I took over the two gun position partially prepared by the 27th T.H.B. which I am relieving, and arranged there having my lighter guns. This afternoon I accompanied the O.C. of the out-going 27th T.H.B. on a kind of inspection of this two gun position on the West of the YPRES Canal but found there unsuitable owing to the great range of this fuse. Reference B.E.GUM. ("B" Series) Sheet 28.N.W. | J.H.L. 29/7/15. O.C. 40 T.H.B. |
|  | 29/7/15 | 10 p.m. | The day was spent in reconnoitring preparing gun positions for the remaining two guns on the  Defence of the YPRES CANAL. | J.H.L. 29/7/15 O.C. 40 T.H.B. |

Army Form C. 2118

# WAR DIARY
## or
## INTELLIGENCE SUMMARY
*(Erase heading not required.)*

40th Trench Mortar Bty

Instructions regarding War Diaries and Intelligence Summaries are contained in F.S. Regs., Part II. and the Staff Manual respectively. Title Pages will be prepared in manuscript.

| Place | Date | Hour | Summary of Events and Information | Remarks and references to Appendices |
|---|---|---|---|---|
| | 30/7 | 9 p.m. | This evening I ranged on enemy trenches, firing six rounds. A.W. 2/L. O.C. 40.T.H.B. | |
| | 31/7 | 10 p.m. | This evening I opened fire on the enemy's first and second line trenches in reply to gun fire on the battalion headquarters. The enemy's trench-mortars replied, but upon the Belgian artillery joining in their fire ceased. I fired nine rounds. A.W. 2/L. O.C. 40.T.M.B. | M.25/15 |

# WAR DIARY or INTELLIGENCE SUMMARY

**Army Form C. 2118**

| Place | Date | Hour | Summary of Events and Information | Remarks and references to Appendices |
|---|---|---|---|---|
| Near VERBRAN-DENMOLEN South of YPRES. | 2nd [Aug] | 4.10 p.m. | At 4 p.m. this afternoon I opened fire on the enemy's advance trench (to counteract), to test the range, with heavy bombs, and provoked a trench-mortar combat lasting about an hour and a half. The enemy replied with bombs first on our advance infantry trench on the right and subsequently lengthening his range tried to hit our gun positions in the rear; without success. Meanwhile further enemy mortars opened on the left with considerable effect, damaging the front parapet, causing several casualties, and very nearly securing direct hits on the left-hand gun position itself. I replied all along the line, securing hits on the right on the enemy's front parapet, and on two prominent points in their rear, but I was unable to reply. | |

reply effectively on the left owing to the extreme oblique position from which the enemy's bombs were coming and the small traverse (20° either side of Zero) provided on my guns (V.S.M. 1½'). I had therefore to content myself with replying on their front line trenches immediately within range. I continued fire until I had expended 20 rounds, when the opposite fire slackening I ceased firing in view of the danger of expending too much ammunition.

The left-hand gun which came dangerously near being put out of action, was at once removed from its position, and will be mounted in its alternative position, already under construction, when that

That is Completed. I showed and that the Belgian artillery joined by efforts to subdue the German mortars on the left, but from report it appears doubtful whether their aid was altogether welcome, as some damage seems to have resulted to our own line.

My observations on this little affair are:

1. The futility of provoking a contest with a limited supply of ammunition.

2. That the policy of trench mortar batteries should, so far as possible, be defensive rather than provocative, so long as ammunition remains limited.

3. The necessity of having a great number of alternative gun positions.

A.T. 7th R.S.F.

**Army Form C. 2118**

# WAR DIARY
## or
## INTELLIGENCE SUMMARY

(Erase heading not required.)

Instructions regarding War Diaries and Intelligence Summaries are contained in F. S. Regs., Part II. and the Staff Manual respectively. Title Pages will be prepared in manuscript.

| Place | Date | Hour | Summary of Events and Information | Remarks and references to Appendices |
|---|---|---|---|---|
| Vorbran devoule | 5/8/15 | 4pm | "B" Wheeare has 10-day handed over charge of 40. T.H.B. acting under orders to report to new B/Battery. | |

[signature]
"L" Res
O.C. 40 T.H.B'y.

1875 Wt. W593/826 1,000,000 4/15 J.B.C. & A. A.D.S.S./Forms/C. 2118.

# WAR DIARY
or
## INTELLIGENCE SUMMARY

Army Form C. 2118

| Place | Date | Hour | Summary of Events and Information | Remarks and references to Appendices |
|---|---|---|---|---|
| Yevlevan Alexunder S.9/pm | 8/8/15 | 8 pm | During the nights of 7/8 & 8/15 and day of the 8th we have been engaged making a new gun position. Have good reason to believe that this may be moved with effect shortly | |

A.L. Duncan Major
O.C. 4o T.H.B.

40th Trench Mortar Battery

Army Form C. 2118.

40 T.T.M.B+y

**WAR DIARY**
or
**INTELLIGENCE SUMMARY**
(Erase heading not required.)

Instructions regarding War Diaries and Intelligence Summaries are contained in F. S. Regs., Part II. and the Staff Manual respectively. Title Pages will be prepared in manuscript.

| Place | Date | Hour | Summary of Events and Information | Remarks and references to Appendices |
|---|---|---|---|---|
| Near Yserrendyke under Sp.4p. | 8/8/15 | | Acting on instructions from Bde. HQ. Quarles & self emplaced a gun emplacement of the East bank of the Canal. At 2-45 we opened fire in conjunction with the artillery. The bombardment lasted about an hour. Unfortunately after firing 9 rounds the gun arm but not actor being fixed by a deep sweep gave it. The gun was undamaged but we had some casualties. In this case we were much handicapped by having to the gun had to be placed in the firing line to be effective and in this case became an easy target for the enemy. He had no casualties. | |
| | 9/8/15 | | Acting on urgent orders we bombarded the enemy's trenches on the N side of the canal. The bombardment opened about 6 p.m. and lasted throughout the night at frequent intervals till 4-30 a.m. Much damage was caused by our stoptpins which easily had the better of the enemy. We | |

1875  Wt. W593/826  1,000,000  4/15  J.B.C. & A.  A.D.S.S./Forms/C. 2118.

Army Form C. 2118

40th Tunnel Howitzer Battery

# WAR DIARY
## or
## INTELLIGENCE SUMMARY
*(Erase heading not required.)*

Instructions regarding War Diaries and Intelligence Summaries are contained in F. S. Regs., Part II. and the Staff Manual respectively. Title Pages will be prepared in manuscript.

| Place | Date | Hour | Summary of Events and Information | Remarks and references to Appendices |
|---|---|---|---|---|
| Wagonlijn Vlamertinghe Molen | Aug 10 | | [illegible handwritten entry] | |
| | Aug 11 | | [illegible handwritten entry] | |
| | Aug 12 | | [illegible handwritten entry] | |
| | Aug 13 | | [illegible handwritten entry] | |
| | Aug 14 | | [illegible handwritten entry] | |

**WAR DIARY**
or
**INTELLIGENCE SUMMARY**

(Erase heading not required.)

Army Form C. 2118

| Place | Date | Hour | Summary of Events and Information | Remarks and references to Appendices |
|---|---|---|---|---|
| Verbranden-molen | 16.6.15 | | At 1 P.m. Enemy fired about seven mortar bombs on our front. No damage. At 5.30 P.m. opened fire on Enemy's trench opposite 31 was about their mortar as ordered by Brigade. Then after three light bombs to draw their mortar a number of rounds fired think heavy and three light bombs returned. | |
| - do - | 17.6.15 | | Under order of Brigade fired at 2 P.m. to draw enemy's mortar fired seven rounds, no was a dud. Drew the Enemy strafed two between 5.P.m. and 7P.m. to fire a saluve to enemy strafed nothing happened. | |
| - do - | 18.6.15 | | Commenced to build Emplacement in 34 Trench. Did not fire. | |
| - do - | 19.6.15 | | Did not fire this date. | |
| - do - | 20.6.15 | | Opened fire at 7 P.m. at enemy's trench opposite 29. Enemy replied but continued the fire till they ceased | |
| - do - | 21.6.15 | | In accordance with Brigade orders opened fire at 1.30 P.m. damaged enemy's rampart. Fired five heavy and thirteen light bombs. Enemy replied vigorously. | |

H.M.Pirolin S.C.
M.O. T. J.4. Y.B.

31/5/15

# WAR DIARY
## or
## INTELLIGENCE SUMMARY
*(Erase heading not required.)*

Army Form C. 2118

| Place | Date | Hour | Summary of Events and Information | Remarks and references to Appendices |
|---|---|---|---|---|
| Vermelles | August 23rd | | Fired no rounds | |
| " | August 24th | | do. do. | |
| " | 25th | | Handed over two 15" Howitzers complete to OC 201 Siege B | |
| " | 26th | | Received two 15" Howitzers from OC 505 S.H.B. | |
| Something (Sweet?) | 26th | | | |
| do | 27th | | About 6.30 PM fired some light bursts from 15.2 French Howitzer Emergency Trench bridge for topping Enemy trench opposite 15.2 to watter in Valley between Hu... | |
| do | 28th | | At 6 P.M opened fire with Howitzers on hut of 15.2 and 15.3 (Shelter sheds) in Sunken Road of landing castle in trench in front of 15.2. 300 rounds fired. Ammunition handed in front of 15.2 to S... Enemy Ammunition... dead. | |
| do | 29th | | Refrained from firing | |

J. A. J. Preston 2/Lt
A.O. F. 1 H. B

Army Form C. 2118

# WAR DIARY
## or
## INTELLIGENCE SUMMARY  40 T [Heavy?] Battery

(Erase heading not required.)

Instructions regarding War Diaries and Intelligence Summaries are contained in F.S. Regs., Part II. and the Staff Manual respectively. Title Pages will be prepared in manuscript.

| Place | Date | Hour | Summary of Events and Information | Remarks and references to Appendices |
|---|---|---|---|---|
| Sanctuary Wood | 30/8/15 | | No firing. Commenced work on new gun position ordered by 3rd Bde | |
| | 31/8/15 | | Work in progress on above | |
| | 1/9/15 | | Work in progress on above. Lt Duncan relieves Lt Preston | |
| | 2/9/15 | | Work in progress " " " | |
| | 3/9/15 | | Work suspended owing to flood caused by rain | |
| | 4/9/15 | | One of position's in progress abandoned and new one to replace it commenced on | 20/9/15 |
| | 5/9/15 | | Shelled out of an old position in B4. Position altered and several rounds fired to register it. Enemy did not reply. Old gun position in B7. partially destroyed by heavy shell. Renewed and improved on. | |

H Duncan Lt.
for O.C. 40 T.H.B.

# WAR DIARY
## or
## INTELLIGENCE SUMMARY

Army Form C. 2118

| Place | Date | Hour | Summary of Events and Information | Remarks and references to Appendices |
|---|---|---|---|---|
| Sanctuary Wood | 6/9/15 | | Enemy fired with his heavy trench Mortars. Retaliated by firing several rounds from three of our Trench Mortars obg't damage done to his trenches. Enemy to this superior range he was able to cause us some inconvenience when he had to be attacked with shelling his trenches. Enemy's rate of fire is very slow and would probably be silenced with larger range mortars. | |
| | 7/9/15 | | Work again in progress on new positions previously mentioned. | |
| | 8/9/15 | | Three O.P.'s were completed and the last one commenced on. | |
| | 9/9/15 | | Lt. Preston relieves Lt. Bruce as fwg. | |
| | 10/9/15 | | Work proceeding in new positions. | |
| | 11/9/15 | | " " " " | |
| | 12/9/15 | | Another gun bed put down in B4. | |

20/9/15

H. Kitson Cpt. R.E.
I/c H.Q. 40 T.M. Bty

Army Form C. 2118

# WAR DIARY
or
## INTELLIGENCE SUMMARY
(Erase heading not required.)

| Place | Date | Hour | Summary of Events and Information | Remarks and references to Appendices |
|---|---|---|---|---|
| Sanctuary Wood | 13/9/15 | | Fired several rounds for registration. Enemy replied with his heavy T. Mortars. He meanwhile vigorously shelling our trenches and causing a fire. Owing to enemy's superior range, it is quite impossible to silence him with mortar fire, answered nevertheless by superior volume of fire | |
| | 14/9/15 | | Work on B7 + B6 in progress | |
| | 15/9/15 | | New magazine for ammunition under construction | |
| | 16/9/15 | | Magazine completed | |
| | 17/9/15 | | Fired C.T. + new Int. gun positions started on | |
| | 18/9/15 | | Work on C.T. in progress | |
| | 19/9/15 | | Rebuilding men's dug outs destroyed during bombardment. | 22/9 |

W.J. Dwyer
2 Lt. R.A.
2nd T.M.B.

# WAR DIARY
## or
## INTELLIGENCE SUMMARY
*(Erase heading not required.)*

Army Form C. 2118

Instructions regarding War Diaries and Intelligence Summaries are contained in F.S. Regs., Part II. and the Staff Manual respectively. Title Pages will be prepared in manuscript.

| Place | Date | Hour | Summary of Events and Information | Remarks and references to Appendices |
|---|---|---|---|---|
| Sanctuary Wood | 20/9/15 | | Working on gun position. All work had to be suspended owing to very heavy artillery fire. Four men were wounded. | |
| | 21/9/15 | | Fired 26 rounds during an artillery actions. Object was to have enemy front charge debris in front of enemy trenches. Bomb throw or at that point apparently not much change. Stopped by infantry to shut firing. Three enemy shells burst inside battle cupola. Removed fuses and detonators and offered them to be cleared as expert ammunition. These were of the same type. 4.5" dia. by 16" long, not approx 60 lbs. At the end with fuse attached to make 8 lbs. | |
| | 22/9/15 | | Fired 20 rounds & cut wire etc. Registered on new position. | |
| | 23/9/15 | | Did not fire. Engaged in strengthening our new gun positions on BC. | |
| | 24/9/15 | | Keeping up ammunition & preparing generally for attack. Built a strong shelter for the men. | |
| | 25/9/15 | | General attack by enemy trenches. Fired 150 rounds during bombardment. Later engaged Hollebeke road. Attempted to put a gun in forward position but attempt had to be abandoned. Gun & all gun positions were destroyed and three men wounded. | |
| | 26/9/15 | | Supply of ammunition from gun positions depots and for stores ammunition pits which were destroyed. | |

Lt Duncan Syces
No. 40 T.M. Bty.

Army Form C. 2118

# WAR DIARY
## or
## INTELLIGENCE SUMMARY
*(Erase heading not required.)*

Instructions regarding War Diaries and Intelligence Summaries are contained in F.S. Regs., Part II. and the Staff Manual respectively. Title Pages will be prepared in manuscript.

| Place | Date | Hour | Summary of Events and Information | Remarks and references to Appendices |
|---|---|---|---|---|
| Sanctuary Wood | Oct 4th | | Nothing of importance occurred today | |
| | Oct 5th | | Old gun position abandoned and new one commenced on | |
| | Oct 6th | | Work proceeding as above | |
| | Oct 7th | | Gun position now completed. We have not registered them as yet. Inf. Bde. only want us to fire in "retaliation" on enemy S.A. gun emplacements. No S.O.S. trenches at present. | |
| | Oct 8th | | No S.O.S. trench action or such all | |
| | Oct 9th | | New dug out for Battery in progress | |
| | Oct 10th | | Work on above in progress | |

14/10/15

J. Bowen Lt R.A.
O.C. 40 F.M.B.

# WAR DIARY
## or
## INTELLIGENCE SUMMARY

Army Form C. 2118

**40th Brigade R.F.A. Battery**

| Place | Date | Hour | Summary of Events and Information | Remarks and references to Appendices |
|---|---|---|---|---|
| A.S. | 1/11/15 | | Hohenzollern position reported last week has been continued. Lt. Buchanan relieves Lt. Duncan. | |
| Map X.28 | 2/11/15 | | All lying low. No aeroplane or observation where it is noticed. | |
| T.19 a.3.10 | 3/11/15 | | Very few shell explosions. Patrol took photograph. Strong a short period only seen were to become most. | |
| | 4/11/15 | | Hohenzollern again commenced damage caused by our artillery to be no possible. Enemy had shown much activity though. The day which has called or attached a detonation on our fired. The firing of 30 rounds on an expended fused apparently however. The enemy and troops were indication. Heavy artillery of enemy answered our firing in a short period. This was the gate Hohenzollern. Gone activities on the works mainly Hohenzollern. Some shots we 32 nd T.M. B.g. pilfered on the present position. The 32 nd T.M. B.g. pilfered. 40 T.M. B.g. which is now completely on our left. Commanded with Rgd. actions and Gen. Battles and Chuze Range. | |
| | 6/11/15 | | Enemy work in and Chuze Range | |
| | 7/11/15 | | | |

Army Form C. 2118.

40 Trench Mortar Battery

# WAR DIARY
## or
## INTELLIGENCE SUMMARY

(Erase heading not required.)

Instructions regarding War Diaries and Intelligence Summaries are contained in F. S. Regs., Part II. and the Staff Manual respectively. Title Pages will be prepared in manuscript.

| Place | Date | Hour | Summary of Events and Information | Remarks and references to Appendices |
|---|---|---|---|---|
| Trench | 7/11/15 | 7 am | Routine Work | |
| " | 8/11/15 | 9.30 am | The Officers, N.C.O's and men of the Battery attended a course of Instruction in Hand Grenades, at the 17th Divisional Bombing School | |
| " | 9/11/15 | 9.30 am | The Battery attended Bombing Course | |
| " | 10/11/15 | 7 am | Routine Work | |
| " | 10/11/15 | 4 pm | One Section goes up to the Trenches Sanctuary Wood, to relieve a section of the 27th Battery | |
| In action | 11/11/15 | — | The Battery is attached to the 9th Division | 18/11 |
| " | 12/11/15 | — | Routine Work. | |
| " | 13/11/15 | — | Routine Work | |

S.G. Bucklerne of
O.C. 40th Trench Mortar Battery

1875 Wt. W593/826 1,000,000 4/15 J.B.C. & A. A.D.S.S./Forms/C. 2118.

# WAR DIARY
or
## INTELLIGENCE SUMMARY

*(Erase heading not required.)*

Army Form C. 2118

| Place | Date | Hour | Summary of Events and Information | Remarks and references to Appendices |
|---|---|---|---|---|
| " | 19/9/15 | 11 am | The German infantry and artillery started a rapid fire which lasted about half an hour, we fired at their trenches during this period | |
| | | 5.30am | The Germans again started some rapid fire with artillery which lasted until about 7.30 am and were firing their own time and some damage to several dugouts by J.P. Duncan and the enemy fired the Grange Garner | |

G.H. Backhouse Lt
for O.C. 40 T.M Battery

40th Siege [Batty?] Mountain [Artillery?]
16/3/–

# WAR DIARY
## or
## INTELLIGENCE SUMMARY
(Erase heading not required.)

Army Form C. 2118

| Place | Date | Hour | Summary of Events and Information | Remarks and references to Appendices |
|---|---|---|---|---|
| 7S | 29th | | In the sector we have just taken over they is only one division T.M. position prepared. This gun is in a thorn wood hedge and enfilades the enemy fire trenches for a distance of 300 yds. Three other places have been selected & work has been started on these. | |
| | 30th | | The three beds have now been fixed in position and temporary shelters prepared for working them. Our second division gun emplacement has also the advantage of enfilading another sector of enemy fire trenches over a distance of 300 yds. The guns are all in emplacements have been chosen from defense rather than offensive work. They are capable of firing both. | |
| | 1st. | | The enemy's Minen Bombs in this sector are all of the cast iron type with both through the entire weight from 12 to 114 lbs. It have its had a large percentage of blinds. Located T.M. and mounted it with the 60 pdr. It be not fired from trenches. We registered with our other T.M.'s and answered light trench fire on his fire trenches. | |
| | 2nd | | to say we have been able to make good progress with the work on hand. Our present enemy has an abundance of T.M. activity in either case. | |
| | 3rd | | I wonder these have been no T.M. activity in either case. Quiet morning we allowed no sound fire. I investigated with enemy has been long too hard to his front line where he has two men of this dug outs. Spent the afternoon in our [N.H?] | |

# WAR DIARY
## or
## INTELLIGENCE SUMMARY.
(Erase heading not required)

Army Form C. 2118.

Instructions regarding War Diaries and Intelligence Summaries are contained in F. S. Regs., Part II. and the Staff Manual respectively. Title pages will be prepared in manuscript.

| Place | Date | Hour | Summary of Events and Information | Remarks and references to Appendices |
|---|---|---|---|---|
| In field | 6/12/15 | 6 am | Opened fire with M. gun in search of a hostile gun, but failed to obtain any retaliation from him. The remainder of the day was spent working on the new emplacement for the same gun. | |
| " | | 6 pm | Lt Barkhouse was relieved by Lt Duncan | |
| " | 7/8/9/12/15 | | We did not fire. In the morning the T.M.C. 5" Gun paid a visit to the trenches. They were working on the emplacements and ammunition dugout the whole day. | |
| " | 9/12/15 | 10.30 am | The enemy started to fire a mortar we retaliated at once firing at the spot from where his bombs came. We fired several rounds and finally silenced him | |
| " | | 3 pm | We continued with the Belgian Artillery in harassing fire on the enemy's front line of trenches. This bombardment appeared to be quite successful. | |
| " | 10/12/15 | | In the morning the T.M.C. 9.2 Dcm again visited the trenches. Party of Sharles in our ammunition dug-outs. Borrowed a carrying party from the King's Own Regt to bring up ammunition from 76 2 Hvy Bde H.Q. We did not fire. | |

Army Form C. 2118.

# WAR DIARY
## or
## INTELLIGENCE SUMMARY.
(Erase heading not required.)

Instructions regarding War Diaries and Intelligence Summaries are contained in F. S. Regs., Part II. and the Staff Manual respectively. Title pages will be prepared in manuscript.

| Place | Date | Hour | Summary of Events and Information | Remarks and references to Appendices |
|---|---|---|---|---|
| In Field | 11/12/15 | | heard 6" gun to its new emplacement an registered it on the German front line of trenches. | |
| " | 12/12/15 | | In the morning we stood by for a bombardment to start by our Heavies but it was postponed until the next day | |

S.M.Wodehouse Lt
for OC M E TM Battery

Army Form C. 2118

# WAR DIARY
or
# INTELLIGENCE SUMMARY

(Erase heading not required.)

Instructions regarding War Diaries and Intelligence Summaries are contained in F.S. Regs., Part II. and the Staff Manual respectively. Title Pages will be prepared in manuscript.

| Place | Date | Hour | Summary of Events and Information | Remarks and references to Appendices |
|---|---|---|---|---|
| Yub | 15/4/15 | 8am | All our guns cooperated with the Belgian Field Artillery and British Heavy Artillery in a bombardment on the enemies front line of trench, we apparently did considerable damage to our target. For the remainder of the day we worked on our first gun emplacement which had sunk in the mud & Doreen has now started on weeks garage ours. | |
| " | 16/4/15 | — | We worked on the enlargement of emplacements. In the evening our store dugout was blown in by a shell. | |
| " | 17/4/15 | — | We pulled down the old store dugout & collected material for a new one. Started to rebuild the dugout | |
| " | 18/4/15 | — | Ditto | |
| " | 19/4/15 | 10.50 | We were prepared to join in with the artillery in a bombardment of the German trenches only it was cancelled owing | |

Army Form C. 2118

WK3/1/16

**WAR DIARY**
or
**INTELLIGENCE SUMMARY**  40th Trench Mortar Battery

(Erase heading not required.)

Instructions regarding War Diaries and Intelligence Summaries are contained in F.S. Regs., Part II. and the Staff Manual respectively. Title Pages will be prepared in manuscript.

| Place | Date | Hour | Summary of Events and Information | Remarks and references to Appendices |
|---|---|---|---|---|
| A.S. | 20/12/15 | | Routine work, draining, and intn. new top store "E" Section relieves "B" Section | |
| | 21/12/15 | | Work in progress on new top store, also on a new gun position | |
| | 22/12/15 | | Work in progress on above. Routine work | |
| | 23/12/15 | | Both new completed. Work on new gun pos'n in progress | |
| | 24/12/15 | | Routine work. Work on above | |
| | 25/12/15 | | Quiet | |
| | 26/12/15 | | Routine work. Work on above. Fired on enemy work artillery. This was our first opportunity of using new 1½ in rifled bomb thrower we had as I think, from experience gained, one dozen fired too recklessly indeed rounds. (of twenty 2 inch bombs fired too recklessly. Enemy T.M.'s have been silent for their absence during the last few weeks. He apparently does not like our 60 pounder which has produced a good deal more effect chiefly any to its precedings I think. | |

J.J. Duncan Lt R.A.
O.C. 40 T.M. Bty

Army Form C. 2118

# WAR DIARY
## or
## INTELLIGENCE SUMMARY
*(Erase heading not required.)*

Instructions regarding War Diaries and Intelligence Summaries are contained in F. S. Regs., Part II. and the Staff Manual respectively. Title Pages will be prepared in manuscript.

| Place | Date | Hour | Summary of Events and Information | Remarks and references to Appendices |
|---|---|---|---|---|
| | Mon 28th Sept-bar | | Work proceeding on our new gun position. No T.M. batteries went as above. Fired several rounds on retaliation. Enemy is most seldom aggressive with his T.M.s. | |
| | Wed 29th | | Work as above. We had again another opportunity of firing the gravity of new T.M. bombing. Up to the period 3 T.M. N.F. was satisfactory. Twelve rounds were fired without any slands. | |
| | Thurs 30th | | 13 gun without any slands. The dug-out shown below on our new position is now complete. It is very strong and is built within an old dug-out. Extra i— with gas. It is hoped that it will be capable of withstanding a German 10 cm. shell. Today we witnessed up a heavy Artillery bombardment of the German Trenches with a T.M. bombardment in the afternoon. A number of rounds fired on tank area was about 10 a.m. bolt bombs caused a great deal of annoyance on the enemy lines. Our large dug-out was destroyed. | |
| | Fri 31st | | A number of places the wire netting in dug-out and above of this front has never been ... | |

1875 W¹: W593/826 1,000,000 4/15 J.B.C. & A. A.D.S.S./Forms/C. 2118.

3
4.0 Trench Mortar Bty
Jan 19/16
Sol VII

40th Trench Mortar Bty

**WAR DIARY** or **INTELLIGENCE SUMMARY**
(Erase heading not required.)

Army Form C. 2118

WO/3/1/16

Instructions regarding War Diaries and Intelligence Summaries are contained in F.S. Regs., Part II. and the Staff Manual respectively. Title Pages will be prepared in manuscript.

| Place | Date | Hour | Summary of Events and Information | Remarks and references to Appendices |
|---|---|---|---|---|
| At Feb [?] | | | Nothing of interest has occurred. We have been chiefly employed in keeping our gun positions in repair. | |
| " | 3rd | | To-day we registered the gunner near position first of all making sure that two of our other guns were ready to open up on the enemy trenches to retaliate. One of our two 2nd guns has been detailed to deal with enemy mortars. One of the enemy mortars which retaliated was silenced by this gun, while another known gun was probably prevented from firing owing to the literal amount of attention which it received. Our shoot was most successful. Two dugouts were seen to cap and a large quantity of the enemy hostile wire and blown back into our own trenches. A large breach was also made in their parapet by two of those shell placed shots from the gun. The firing of the guns has now been a pleasure owing to the very small percentage of mishaps we now have. Of the 40 rounds we fired 25 were read with 8 [?] and | |

# WAR DIARY
## or
## INTELLIGENCE SUMMARY

Army Form C. 2118

(Erase heading not required.)

Instructions regarding War Diaries and Intelligence Summaries are contained in F. S. Regs., Part II. and the Staff Manual respectively. Title Pages will be prepared in manuscript.

| Place | Date | Hour | Summary of Events and Information | Remarks and references to Appendices |
|---|---|---|---|---|
| In the Field | Jan 3rd | | The remaining 15 were No much more of which were blinds. Enemy was evidently badly damaged as he retaliated on us furiously with his heavy field guns. The damage done to us was however nil. | |
| " " " | " 4th | | We did not fire but worked on our emplacements | |
| " " " | " 5th | | ditto | |
| " " " | " 6th | | Lt Duncan was relieved by 2nd Lt Balham. | |
| " " " | " 7th | | Today we combined with the Artillery in bombarding the hostile trenches for two hours during which we fired 56 rounds and had no blinds at all, but we had five bad detonations. There was very considerable damage done to the enemy and to his trenches, one of our guns succeeded in absolutely demolishing one of their observation posts. We have not fired today but have been busy working on a new emplacement for one of our Krupp guns | |

1875 Wt. W593/826 1,000,000 4/15 J.B.C. & A. A.D.S.S./Forms/C. 2118.

(signed) V.G. Brewer /Capt/
O.C. 2nd K T.M. Battery (2nd T.M.C.)

Army Form C. 2118.

# WAR DIARY
## or
## INTELLIGENCE SUMMARY.
(Erase heading not required.)

Instructions regarding War Diaries and Intelligence Summaries are contained in F.S. Regs., Part II. and the Staff Manual respectively. Title pages will be prepared in manuscript.

| Hour, Date, Place | Summary of Events and Information | Remarks and references to Appendices |
|---|---|---|
| In the field Jan 2. 8 | We have not fired to-day but have been working on two of our emplacements | |
| " " 10 A | This morning we fired at a sniper's post in their front line trenches, a very large column of smoke poured out of the trench, where one of our shots first, for a very long time afterwards, we very probably lit a gas cylinder. | |
| " " 11 ½ | This afternoon our 4ᵗʰ at the enemy's line of dug-outs we could see for ourselves that we did a great deal of damage, a large number of our shots burst upon the sausage timbers or corrugated iron | |
| " " 12 ½ | We have not been firing to-day but have been | |

Army Form C. 2118.

# WAR DIARY
## or
## INTELLIGENCE SUMMARY.
*(Erase heading not required.)*

Instructions regarding War Diaries and Intelligence Summaries are contained in F.S. Regs., Part II. and the Staff Manual respectively. Title pages will be prepared in manuscript.

| Hour, Date, Place | Summary of Events and Information | Remarks and references to Appendices |
|---|---|---|

In the Field Jan 13th — working on the drainage of our emplacements. To-day we fired at a line of dugouts in the enemy support line of trenches & succeed in blowing up a good deal of roofing material.

14th "We did not fire to day", worked on ammunition dug-out.

15th This morning we coöperated with the Belgian Artillery in a bombardment of the enemy front line of trenches doing considerable damage to their dugouts.

P.R. Butcher Lt
2nd⁄2 T.M. Battery

Army Form C. 2118

# WAR DIARY
## or
## INTELLIGENCE SUMMARY
*(Erase heading not required.)*

| Place | Date | Hour | Summary of Events and Information | Remarks and references to Appendices |
|---|---|---|---|---|
| In the Field | Jan 15 | | Lieut Afflin relieved Lieut Backhouse. In the afternoon our fires on our artillery observation post. | |
| " | " 16 | | To-day I moved C gun out of its position, and started to make an emplacement just behind the extreme left of I 34 support trench. | |
| " | " 17 | | We fired at I 34 & 3 and did some considerable damage. In the morning the T.M.C. visited the trenches | |
| " | " 18 | | We fired again at I 34 & 33 and destroyed the work which they had done during the night. "A" gun (two inch) was taken out of action and sent back to billets | |
| " | " 19 | | At 11 a.m. the infantry were cleared out of the front trenches, and fire was opened by 8 howitzers Belgian batteries 40 & 43½ French Light Batteries on the enemies redoubt, one of our guns was turned on a point at I 34 d 24 and our two 1½ inch batteries guns at I 34 & 16. We could see trenches that were did a great deal of damage to the enemy's trench. | |
| " | " 20 | | T.M.C. went round the trenches. We opened fire with one gun on the | |

1875 Wt. W593/826 1,000,000 4/15 J.B.C. & A. A.D.S.S./Forms/C. 2118.

# WAR DIARY
## or
## INTELLIGENCE SUMMARY

Army Form C. 2118

| Place | Date | Hour | Summary of Events and Information | Remarks and references to Appendices |
|---|---|---|---|---|
| In the Field | Jan 21 | | enemy salient at I 34 c 95 and on his front line of trenches, blowing the roofs of two dug-outs into the air. L/C Backhouse relieved L/ A. Phin.<br>In the afternoon we fired at I 34 d x 7 which was a machine gun emplacement we obtained one direct hit which blew it to pieces. | |

Ptd. Backhouse L/
40 E T.M. Battery
3rd Div.

# WAR DIARY
## or
## INTELLIGENCE SUMMARY

Army Form. C. 2118

Instructions regarding War Diaries and Intelligence Summaries are contained in F.S. Regs., Part II. and the Staff Manual respectively. Title Pages will be prepared in manuscript.

| Place | Date | Hour | Summary of Events and Information | Remarks and references to Appendices |
|---|---|---|---|---|
| In the field | Oct 11th | | Engaged in strengthening the front of trenches occupied. Quiet day did not fire upon Mr Gunman Smith was observed at night by Lgt Summit in the trenches | |
| | 12th | | Quiet during day did not fire. About 6pm enemy commenced bombarding redoubt lasted for one hour. Cpl. O. MacKay R.S.F. was slightly wounded, he was sent to dressing dept. Mr Arthur proceeded on leave. | |
| | 13th | | Quiet day did not fire. At night the big guns not in action were taken off. Searching wood with 52 Rds complete by Orders from B.H.Q. | |
| | 14th | | Engaged in preparing line suitable positions near Big French ox'th turn in action by noon, did not fire. | |
| | 15th | | Engaged in making positions strong during the morning at noon was going to regiment with both teams but received orders not to fire. Mr Duncan being in charge the gunners Smith returned after a month or my Mr ... | |
| | 16th | | ... | |

# WAR DIARY
## or
## INTELLIGENCE SUMMARY
*(Erase heading not required.)*

Army Form C. 2118

| Place | Date | Hour | Summary of Events and Information | Remarks and references to Appendices |
|---|---|---|---|---|
| Sanctuary Wood | 18/10/15 | | Routine work. Work commenced on a new dug-out for the new gun. | |
| | 19/10/15 | | Continued | |
| | 20/10/15 | | Continuation. 2nd Lieut Duncan relieves Lt Ward | |
| | 21/10/15 | | One new gun position commenced on right of 3rd T.M.B. New position for two 1½" guns has been commenced in. This position is now in defensive state. Offensive purposes and is being made very strong. | |
| | 22/10/15 | | Work proceeding on shelf emplacements | |
| | 23/10/15 | | Trench and tunneling party where a lot of night has been proceeding lately was interrupted by an important incident. Shell which bursted in a barn and a H.E. gun artillery commenced with no shelling enemy C.T.'s. No cases struggles and searching for every T.M. batteries. As far as can be ascertained, the damage was average. Today towards first 52. of the 21 steady gun was trained 7 were behind of the 14 gun and a half inch fired it was behind the gun left gun fired 13 rounds without any thirds. We had 8 was fired. Work was also continued on new position movement above | Note R.T.M. Group 3rd HQ of 1, 2, 3rd, 4th & 5th T.M. B's |
| | 24/10/15 | | | |

A. Duncan 2nd Lt
O.C. R.T.M. Group 3

# WAR DIARY or INTELLIGENCE SUMMARY

Army Form C. 2118

(Erase heading not required.)

| Place | Date | Hour | Summary of Events and Information | Remarks and references to Appendices |
|---|---|---|---|---|
| Sanctuary Wood | 11 | | Routine work. Consolidating new position | |
| | 12 | | Fired on retaliation to enemy trench mortars. Quiet on all front. | |
| | 13 | | Enemy very active with trench mortars, bombarded a portion of our trench. He bombarded their position and fired shows to retire. Action lasted at intervals from 6am till 1.30pm. He had many good hits but unfortunately they percent 1½" trench mortars were blind. Altogether this number included some 240 trench fired by 2nd Bty T.M.Bty who at the same time were firing in answer to enemy. A heavy 80lb Trench fired were (even fried) & she has been reported. | |
| | 14 | | Two fem Vict gun 143d T.M.B. have fired R.T.M. Emp another trench Mere for Bn. Position had been selected & work proceeding on emplacement for these guns. Fixed several rounds for 2" gun in retaliation to enemy T.M's | |
| | 15 | | Bombarded an enemy trench supposed to be a minen Shaft. The guns used were 2" and a grey class. Damage cannot yet be ascertained level the forts with exception of one exploded heavily and possibly wounded one hundred. Altogether the fired gun fired garner Registered | |

# WAR DIARY
## or
## INTELLIGENCE SUMMARY
*(Erase heading not required.)*

Army Form C. 2118

| Place | Date | Hour | Summary of Events and Information | Remarks and references to Appendices |
|---|---|---|---|---|
| | 16/9/15 | | Weather & both sides. Gun fire position's being manned when damaged by action of yesterday. | |
| | 17/9/15 | | Nothing to report. Routine work. Field several wires. | |

A.J. Duncan L.R.C.
O.C. 40 T.M. By
and R.T.M. Spots
1st year

R. 9/6/15

1875  Wt. W593/826  1,000,000  4/15  J.B.C. & A.  A.D.S.S./Forms/C. 2118.

### 3RD DIVISION
### DIVL. ARTILLERY

TRENCH MORTAR BATTS.

~~JULY-DEC 1916~~

1916 MAR — 1916 DEC

3rd Divisional Artillery.

Z / 3 TRENCH MORTAR BATTERY.

(late 308th)

MARCH 1916.

Army Form C. 2118

# WAR DIARY
## or
## INTELLIGENCE SUMMARY

(Erase heading not required.)

308th T.M.B.
Z 3

Instructions regarding War Diaries and Intelligence Summaries are contained in F. S. Regs., Part II. and the Staff Manual respectively. Title Pages will be prepared in manuscript.

| Place | Date 1916 | Hour | Summary of Events and Information | Remarks and references to Appendices |
|---|---|---|---|---|
| TOURNEHEM | M&H 1-10 | | Bty in training. | |
| | 11 | | Marched to RENINGHELST. | |
| | 12- | | Took over 40th TMB position at St Eueuds. Worked at repair of positions & salving guns & ammn; much damaged by enemy fire during operations at BLUFF in previous days. | |
| | 16 | | Bty moved to ST ELOI & took up positions in P.trenches. Preparing positions for assault on the MOUND. Registered guns on allotted target. | |
| | 17 | | | |
| | 18- | | | |
| | 24 | | | |
| | 25 | | Relieved by 9th Bde S.M.A.P.E. | |
| | 26-27 | | Explosion of mines at 4.15 am Sunday, Such 27 Jh followed by bombardement. Bty fired 50 S.S. lbs Shrap, 100 bombs Stokes. | |
| | | | 105 STOKES BOMBS. Bn Wilkes & Bn Douglas wounded. | |
| | 28 | | Relieved by 2/U. S.M.A.P.E. | |
| | 29- | | Bty in positions in P.trenches retiring unfaveroubly | |
| | 31 | | cleaning up after battle. Bn CHEW recovered from concussion. | |

J.W. McLean, Captain
308th T.M.B.

Comdg
Z 3

3rd Divisional Artillery.

Z / 3  TRENCH  MORTAR  BATTERY.

(late 308th)

APRIL  1916.

# WAR DIARY
## or
## INTELLIGENCE SUMMARY.

Army Form C. 2118.

Z 3 T.M.Bty Vol

| Place | Date | Hour | Summary of Events and Information | Remarks and references to Appendices |
|---|---|---|---|---|
| | 1916 | | | |
| RENINGHELST | April | | Bty remained in action after the capture of trenches at ST ELOI when handed over to Canadian Div. but did no shooting. It was withdrawn from the line on April 4th & remained in rest at RENINGHELST until April 11th when it moved with the 30th Bde. Amm. Col. to STEENEVOORDE. 2/Lt SNIPE was appointed O.C. X3 T.M.Bty on April 13th and this Bty. left without a sub. officer. Gr. CHEW was awarded the D.C.M. for gallantry & services at ST ELOI on April 25th. | |
| | April 2? | | Bty moved from STEENEVOORDE to farm near KEMMEL previously held by 50th Div. who judging from the T.M positions they handed over do not take much interest in this arm. | |

J Allan Boulton
Lt. RFA
Comdg Z 3 T.M. Bty.

3rd Divisional Artillery.

3RD TRENCH MORTAR BATTERY.

JULY 1916.

Army Form C. 2118.

# WAR DIARY
## or
## INTELLIGENCE SUMMARY

(Erase heading not required.)

3rd Trench Mortar Battery

Instructions regarding War Diaries and Intelligence Summaries are contained in F. S. Regs., Part II. and the Staff Manual respectively. Title Pages will be prepared in manuscript.

| Place | Date | Hour | Summary of Events and Information | Remarks and references to Appendices |
|---|---|---|---|---|
| | 6 | 7.30pm | Marched to Ebergnies | |
| | | | in trained for Doullens | |
| | 4 | 7am | marched for Souller | |
| | | 5am | Schuras | |
| | | 3pm | Marched to Vignacourt | |
| | | 8.30h | Batteries from one of P.A. | |
| | 8 | 10am | Marched to Ganneville | |
| | | | Marched to Franvillers | |
| | 9 | 9.30 | Inspection. Rested for day | |
| | | 2pm | | |
| | 10 | 11.30 | Marched to A.B.C | |
| | | 7pm | A.B.C. H.Q. | |
| | 11 | 9:00 | | |
| | 12 | 9am | | |
| | 13 | | | |
| | 14 | | | |
| | 15 | 8am | Moved to Lozenge Wood | |
| | | 2pm | | |

Army Form C. 2118.

3rd Trench Mortar Battery

# WAR DIARY
## or
## INTELLIGENCE SUMMARY

*(Erase heading not required.)*

Instructions regarding War Diaries and Intelligence Summaries are contained in F. S. Regs., Part II. and the Staff Manual respectively. Title Pages will be prepared in manuscript.

| Place | Date | Hour | Summary of Events and Information | Remarks and references to Appendices |
|---|---|---|---|---|
| In Action | Sept 16th | — | Same position as on 15th | |
| — | 17th | 2 pm | Two guns in Battery removed for action in O.G. Lines left of Brigade. Remaining guns same position as on 16th. | |
| — | 18th | — | Same position as on 17th. 250 bombs (Stokes) fired with good results. | |
| — | — | 9 pm | Relieved by 2nd Brigade T.M.B. Battery in support at Lozenge Wood. | |
| — | 19th | 7 pm | Moved back in reserve to Maese Redoubt. | |
| — | 20th | 6 pm | Moved to billets in Albert – Divisional Reserve. | |
| Albert | 21st | 9-11pm | Raining. | |
| — | 22nd | 6 pm | Marched to Birch Wood in support. Badly shelled between Becourt Wood and Lozenge Wood. | |
| In Action | 23rd | 1 pm | Returned to Albert. | |
| Albert | 24th | 7 am | Marched to bombardment. Two guns immediately placed in action in front line firing on Point 41 Munster Trench. Six guns remained in support at Hippodrome. | |
| In Action | 25th | — | Two guns in the line fired in support of Rebel attack on Point 41 Munster Trench. 2/Lt G.K. George and 1/Cpl Kenneth both badly wounded. | |

Army Form C. 2118.

# WAR DIARY
## or
## INTELLIGENCE SUMMARY  3rd Trench Mortar Battery
(Erase heading not required.)

| Place | Date | Hour | Summary of Events and Information | Remarks and references to Appendices |
|---|---|---|---|---|
| In action | July 26th | — | Two guns in the line were in action in conjunction with Anzacs. One gun buried but afterwards recovered. | |
| | | 9.30p | Relieved by 68th T.M.B. Proceeded forward to Millencourt. | |
| Millencourt | 27th | — | Rest. | |
| " | 28th | — | Rest. | |
| " | 29th | 9a–1p | Training | |
| " | 30th | 10am | Church Parade | |
| " | 31st | 9a–1p | Training | |
| Millencourt | Aug. 1st | 7a–10.30am | Route March and Battery Parade. Training of new men same hours. | |
| | 2nd | 9–10.30p | Infantry and gun training | |
| — | | 4.45p | Inspected by [illegible] G.O.C. 3rd Army Corps | |

3rd Divisional Artillery

"X" "Y" "Z" TRENCH MORTAR BATTERIES

AUGUST 1916

# WAR DIARY
## or
## INTELLIGENCE SUMMARY

*(Erase heading not required.)*

X.3.T.M.B. No. 31st August

August 1916

| Place | Date | Hour | Summary of Events and Information | Remarks and references to Appendices |
|---|---|---|---|---|
| DERNACOURT | 1/8/16 to 14/8/16 | | Battery worked daily on Railway dumps. Packing empty cases into ammunition boxes & loading them into trucks | |
| | 15/8/16 | | Moved to Happy Valley at BRAY, Sur SOMME. | |
| BRAY SUR SOMME | to 20/8/16 | 8pm | Started working on gun positions for 3rd D.A. | |
| | 21/8/16 to 25/8/16 | | Assisted Y.3.T.M.B. to put in a 9.45" Trench Mortar at TRONES WOOD | |
| | 26/8/16 | | Used ammunition as 9.45" T. Mortar. | |
| | 27/8/16 | | | |
| NOEUX LES MINES | 28/8/16 to 29/8/16 30/8/16 to 31/8/16 | | Billeted with men from Béthune & proceeded by lorry to NOEUX les MINES. Inoculation & light fatigues. | 31/8/16 |

## WAR DIARY or INTELLIGENCE SUMMARY

1st – 31st August

| Place | Date | Hour | Summary of Events and Information | Remarks and references to Appendices |
|---|---|---|---|---|
| DERNACOURT | 1/8/16 to 4/8/16 | | August 1916. Daily fatigues on Railway dump. Sorting empty cases & boxes of ammunition & packing same. | Y.3. Trench Mortar B'ty. |
| BRAY sur SOMME | 15/8/16 to 20/8/16 | | Marched to HAPPY VALLEY nr BRAY. Worked on the line for the 3rd D.A. erecting gun positions, etc |  |
| | 21/8/16 | | Helped Y.3 T.M.B. to prepare an emplacement & fire on 9.45" Trench mortar. | |
| | 26/8/16 | | Carried ammunition to 9.45" T.M. etc. | |
| | 29/8/16 | | Battery returned to Happy Valley & proceeded by motor | |
| NOEUX LES MINES | 28/8/16 & 29/8/16 | | lorry to NOEUX LES MINES | |
| | 30/8/16 | | Kit inspections & light camp fatigues | |
| | 31/8/16 | | | |

31/8/16

Lt. y Aylin 2nd
OC Y3 TMB

# WAR DIARY or INTELLIGENCE SUMMARY.

(Erase heading not required.)

L/3 T.M.By. 1st – 31st Aug.

| Place | Date | Hour | Summary of Events and Information | Remarks and references to Appendices |
|---|---|---|---|---|
| Bray Dernancourt | Aug 1st 2nd | | The Battery was employed on fatigues at the A.T.T.B. Bray. Recovery camp to Dernancourt where the By. bivouacked on the edge of the River. | |
| " | 11th 12th 13th " | | The Battery was employed on fatigue at Edge Hill station pulling up railway and communication lines etc | |
| " | 14 " | | Bivouacked at the cross roads between by-pass Bray and Bray where the Battery bivouacked | |
| " | 15 to 27 " | | The Battery was employed on digging gunpits for the eg th By. T.M. Bde on trench Hard Ridge in front of Bouzincourt Q. 32675 South Arrass Wd | |
| " | 28 " | | Relieved on action relief on this fatigue | |
| " | 29 " | | On the afternoon received orders to move to Querrieu Querrieu | |
| " | 30 " | | and the Battery travelled all night to by Army carrying on Arrived at Querrieu at 5 AM the remainder of the 29th to 30th was spent on company stables and resting the men | |

3rd Divisional Artillery.

3RD TRENCH MORTAR BATTERY.

SEPTEMBER 1916.

# WAR DIARY or INTELLIGENCE SUMMARY

| Place | Date | Hour | Summary of Events and Information | Remarks and references to Appendices |
|---|---|---|---|---|
| | 19 | | Medium Batteries went into action in HULLUCH and LOOS, where they relieved 2nd Divisional trench mortars. H.B. Heavy trench mortar Batteries did not arrive in this area until the 23rd, having been trained in the SOMME district. The three medium trench mortar Batteries were greatly together with the 9/k.hv Batteries of the 8 Bde & the 4/th Infantry Brigade. Schemes were discussed by Corps were Battery Commanders and would not available could be obtained to which the dilapidated condition of the enemy were was well testified and the wires withheld remaining. Ancient Gun fire H.B. Heavy trench mortar ammunition from 2-9-16 to 6/3-9-16 was something 9.45" ammunition from 139 Railway Arty and Columns houses etc. on the 12/6-1 on 19/3 nearly burned by hostile M.G. fire added the fact following on the 30-1-39 were used in the light hand pick shell on 13/6 heads. Col. Sutherland joined from 139 Railway Arty and Columns | |

# WAR DIARY or INTELLIGENCE SUMMARY

Army Form C. 2118.

| Place | Date | Hour | Summary of Events and Information | Remarks and references to Appendices |
|---|---|---|---|---|
| contd | | | Lieut. McAlin, 13th Hants - 1/B 3rd Bde in the trenches. The expenditure of ammunition was very high, but would have been more but for the hindrance experienced in the constant blowing out of rifle mechanism. Retaliation on the whole was not very brisk and was invariably tried out by our increased fire. | |
| 24/9/16 to 30/9/16 | | | Brigade proceeded to BLESSY, when Lewis Gun marching, returning and Gas Helmet drills were carried out, instructions in the use of the Lewis Clinometer, and Lectures on various topics were given. | |

E.B. MacLaren Lt
T.M.O. 3rd Bde

3rd Divisional Artillery.

3RD TRENCH MORTAR BATTERY.

OCTOBER 1916.

"Heavy & Medium Trench Mortars," 3rd Div.
1st to 31st Oct 1916. Army Form C. 2118.

Vol 4

# WAR DIARY
or
# INTELLIGENCE SUMMARY

Instructions regarding War Diaries and Intelligence Summaries are contained in F. S. Regs., Part II. and the Staff Manual respectively. Title Pages will be prepared in manuscript.

| Place | Date | Hour | Summary of Events and Information | Remarks and references to Appendices |
|---|---|---|---|---|
| J.S.H. but | 1916 Oct 1st | | X/3 Y/3 & Z/3 Indian Mrtrs. into action. Proceeded by Motor Lorry to COURCELLES. X/3 Proceeded into action at K.03.a K.39 owing to shortage of men on Rations could muster only active personnel, great trouble has been intervals, as previously reported, great trouble has been again experienced owing to the rifle mechanism becoming out, only one invalid carbine fired to being found in any gun being wounded but with the mechanism in Walker. Y/3 keeping in action. 7 O.R. wounded (1.5) of STAFF 20P.S.E. the ammunition trunks at this place secured regular attention from the enemy and finally on the 12th & were blown but flew it up devastating dugouts & boundaries of trenches. 2/Lt APLIN, 13th Hants and 3 O.R. were slightly wounded & badly shaken. Their dugout having fallen in. They remained at duty. Parties not in action were constantly employed on various work at buildings in trenches. X/3 & Z/3 kept at action. |  |
|  | 13th | | until during which a few casualties were incurred but Position was generally very heavy. X/3 36P, Z/13 1 LOR wounded. X/3 2P.B. rifle grans were not in action. X/3 Y/3 & Z/13 out of action after three days march, arrived at COURCELLES not being in action. |  |

Army Form C. 2118.

WAR DIARY
or
INTELLIGENCE SUMMARY

(Erase heading not required.)

| Place | Date | Hour | Summary of Events and Information | Remarks and references to Appendices |
|---|---|---|---|---|

action would attest to this but were in the nature of working parties in the trenches carrying out ing & extensions of various dumps. No reports of enemy action have been frequently held.

3rd Divisional Artillery.

3RD TRENCH MORTAR BATTERY.

NOVEMBER 1916.

# WAR DIARY or INTELLIGENCE SUMMARY

Army Form C. 2118.

Trench Mortar Batteries (Medium & Heavy) 3rd Division
1st to 30th Novr. 1916.

(Erase heading not required.)

| Place | Date | Hour | Summary of Events and Information | Remarks and references to Appendices |
|---|---|---|---|---|
| COURCELLES | 1/11/16 | | Batteries carried out relief at SERRE FRONT, only 2 mortars being in action, the others having been previously withdrawn for cleaning and repairs on account of the fact that the remainder worked on the general movement for easy tactics were also furnished to salvage ammunition from the trenches. A general withdrawal of all mortars in Divisional Sectors was carried out by the 4th Nov. All mortars in ENZ & ENZ2 subs 3 & 4 Sept. L Sub & 6 Sub L Sub & 5 Sub L Sub were relieved from the line. | |
| AU-BOIS | | | On 13th COURCELLES-AU-BOIS was also asked a temporary billet for the entire Group. Orders which the trench of the surface issued to M.O. in accordance with instructions. | |
| | 14/11/16 | | Report issued to Division on the following day. | |
| | 16/11/16 | | Previous number of Jones which are now used to has a canteen shelter & an extra room in 152 [illegible] to the men was removed to be the Railway [illegible] so as to be furnished for food cleaning as 9.F/A arrive the way into huts B(N) Aveluy [illegible] further order. | |
| | 26/11/16 | | Invited for table building for 2/F.A.K. | |
| | | | Received W.O. [illegible] Reg. submitting weekly CORPSE 9 + further 4x/3 am in Novr. A.W. Arne Landing. Also 2 [illegible] are working in new position Doningcourt. | |

T2134. Wt. W708—776. 500000. 4/15. Sir J. C. & S.

T.M.O.
3rd Div.

3rd Divisional Artillery.

3RD TRENCH MORTAR BATTERY.

DECEMBER 1916.

Army Form C. 2118.

Trenches Monture – 3rd Bn.
1st to 31st Decr 1916

# WAR DIARY
or
## INTELLIGENCE SUMMARY
(Erase heading not required.)

| Place | Date | Hour | Summary of Events and Information | Remarks and references to Appendices |
|---|---|---|---|---|
| BOIS EN HACHE – ARTOIS | | | The 3 thousand J.M. Butts were employed in the trenches held by the Bn. Corpse, constructing 2 gun positions and accommodation for personnel. Owing to the state of the trenches which were very bad, and all work being done under difficulties the work was difficult and consequently slow. Four Batteries were employed and worked in relays for the 4th Bn H.L.I. and 15th Bn. H.L.I. and relieved by 116th from in-coming battn. Yellow Rd & Yellow Rta found in trenches selections of Battn. were employed on Arrival [illegible] Bn. H.L.I. & 4th Bn. [illegible] relieved in turn to B.R. and R.E. [illegible] also did some semi-permanent [illegible] for defence. 4th Bn H.L.I. [illegible] to [illegible] & Liggat KRR advanced posts as [illegible] [illegible] Brickfields & at 14th Tmbln in P.Y. Sap. Some extra [illegible] [illegible]. | |
| | 31st 1916 | | Our curtain at K.33. C.25.80 + K.26 b 85.09. The 4 pdr Mg. commenced work on new position – which requires many improvements – and on clearing lines of communications on [illegible] [illegible] [illegible] H.Q. 4th Bn. J.G. Onslow returned from leave & Lieut. B.O. Quinn, BIRD. & E.C. Inglis to returned on leave to U.K. pm 21st [illegible]. Battn. remained in about to the right of Suck [illegible] [illegible] [illegible] remained in trenches. | Trenches No 2 [illegible] No 3 [illegible] |

# WAR DIARY or INTELLIGENCE SUMMARY

**Army Form C. 2118.**

(Erase heading not required.)

| Place | Date | Hour | Summary of Events and Information | Remarks and references to Appendices |
|---|---|---|---|---|
| BUSSEN-<br>DRIES | 1st<br>to<br>3rd. | | Parties proceeded to trenches to continue work. 1 O.R. of X/9/N.12/g was killed by a shell at EUSTON DUMP this place receives particular attention from the enemy.<br><br>As the work was concentrated on digging and construction no events of importance took place only 2 Mortars have been put in action from which 3 rounds were fired for registration purposes. | |

C. Siddall
Capt.
T.M.C. 3'' Div.

3rd Divisional Artillery.

X / 3   Trench Mortar Battery.

J U L Y   1 9 1 6.

Army Form C. 2118

X/3 T.M. Bty
1-31 July 1916

# WAR DIARY
or
# INTELLIGENCE SUMMARY
(Erase heading not required.)

X 3 Trench Mortar Battery

| Place | Date | Hour | Summary of Events and Information | Remarks and references to Appendices |
|---|---|---|---|---|
| | 1/7/16 | | Moving from Wiguens to Doeuve. | |
| | 3/7/16 | | Bois des Tailles. Travaille + inspection of kits + equipment | |
| | 4/7/16 | | | |
| | 5/7/16 | | moved to Bray sur Somme. Battery commenced fatigues in | |
| | 6/7/16 | | trenches. | |
| | 10/7/16 | | Battery working for 142nd Bgde R.F.A. in the trenches. Building | |
| | 10/7/16 | | dugouts, gunpits etc. | |
| | | | No 54120 Bomb. Churchill A. & 9.4.} were wounded on the 20th | |
| | 20/7/16 | | No 58228 Gnr Otter T. Rgt #} | |
| | 20/7/16 | | 2nd Lt Aylin E.J. X 3 T.M.B. was took command of | |
| | | | X 3 T.M.B. | |
| | 20/7/16 | | Fatigues for 3rd D.A.C. on dumps | |
| | 22/7/16 | | | |
| | 24/7/16 | | Fatigues in trenches for 23rd Bgde R.F.A. | |
| | 25/7/16 | | | |
| | 29/7/16 | | Fatigues for 3rd D.A.C. on dumps. | |
| | 31/7/16 | | | |

E.C. Aylin Lt.

3rd Divisional Artillery.

Y / 3  TRENCH MORTAR BATTERY.

J U L Y  1 9 1 6.

# WAR DIARY
## or
## INTELLIGENCE SUMMARY

Army Form C. 2118

Y 3 T.M.B.
1 - 31 July 1916.

| Place | Date | Hour | Summary of Events and Information | Remarks and references to Appendices |
|---|---|---|---|---|
| | 1/7/16 | | Moving from Aveluy to Daours on the 3rd. Battery marched from Bouzin to Daours 23 miles without a single man falling out. Daours gun & equipment overhauled. | Vol 3 |
| | 3/7/16 | | | |
| | 3/7/16 | | | |
| | 5/7/16 | | | |
| | 5/7/16 | | Boo des Tailles. Route march etc. | |
| | 9/7/16 | | | |
| | 10/7/16 | | Battery was in the trenches, doing fatigues for 42nd Bgde R.F.A. | |
| | | | Bridge building, Road mending, Stretcher carrying, etc. | |
| | 19/7/16 | | Lt Batchelor took over TMC from Capt Kelley & took over 8 x 3 | |
| | 20/7/16 | | became OC Y3 Battery. | |
| | 20/7/16 to 31/7/16 | | Fatigues for 3rd D.A.E. Ammunition loading etc. | |

F. J. Afohn 2nd Lt
OC Y 3 T M B

# WAR DIARY
## INTELLIGENCE SUMMARY
*(Erase heading not required).*

Army Form C. 2118.

| Place | Date | Hour | Summary of Events and Information | Remarks and references to Appendices |
|---|---|---|---|---|
| BRAY | Aug 2 | 1 | Moved to Rest area. Battery employed during rest at establishment ammunition dump | |
| DERNANCOURT | 15 | | " Bray. Battery employed in working parties to T.M. Brigade. | |
| BRAY | 16 20 | | | |
| | 20 | | Ordered to place one mortar in action against Guillemont. Finding the impossible in the time given, ordered to withdraw. | |
| TRONES WOOD | 21 31 | | Ordered to start digging emplacement in order to put one mortar into action against Guillemont. Continued working till the end of the month. The mortar was placed in position on the night of the 26/27. with 20 rounds of ammunition. During this period, one man wounded. | |

Duplicate

Lionel Ward 2/Lt
R.F.A.
Cmdg V/5 Hy T.M. Battery

3rd Divisional Artillery.

Z / 3 TRENCH MORTAR BATTERY.

(late 308th)

JULY 1916.

Army Form C. 2118.

Z/3 T.M. Bty
1-31 July 1916

# WAR DIARY
or
# INTELLIGENCE SUMMARY.
(Erase heading not required.)

Instructions regarding War Diaries and Intelligence Summaries are contained in F.S. Regs., Part II. and the Staff Manual respectively. Title pages will be prepared in manuscript.

| Place | Date | Hour | Summary of Events and Information | Remarks and references to Appendices |
|---|---|---|---|---|
| July 1st 1916 St Omer | | | The Battery, after leaving waterlot, was billeted in the Infantry Barracks at Omer pending Entrainment | |
| St Omer | 2.7.16 | | The Batty crossed by 2pm the ZAC to entrain and then motored to Duke Lebon III cont | |
| Doulens | 3.7.16 | | continued themselves from Bir June Bty Belonnes at Doulens and proceeded to Baigneux | |
| | 4 } 5 } | | During the night of the 4th.6th the Bty [not TM Bde] proceeded rations | |
| Daours | 5th | | to Daours vice Officino No. 67415 for C.Smith was transferred to the 50th LIM RGA | |
| | 6th | | While at Daours a draft of 12 men were delivered at the Y3TM Bty | |
| | 7th | | Four men were transferred to X3 TM Bty and four men to Y3TM Bty. | |
| Bois des Taillis | 8.9.16 } | | Proceeded to camp at Bois des Taillis. | |
| Bray | 10th | | Proceeded to camp near Bray | |
| Minden Post | 11th to 20th July | | The Batty was temp attached to 40th Bde RFA for fatigues, communications duties, building etc. No. 37596 Gr Hyde was released to 64th DIV. T.A.H.Q. | |
| | 21st | | Batty returned to TM camp over Bray. Gr HC further camp and communication to | |
| | | | 10342 Gr Carr reported 129 Bty RPA. | |
| Bray | 22nd.23rd | | Cleaned up, overhauled guns, slings etc. Rested its new recruit Lieut Pryce | |
| | 24th Augt | | The Batty was detailed to carry out fatigues for the UAC communication | |
| | | | dump. | |

$+ enemy line Lieut at Z3 TMBty

3rd Divisional Artillery.

V / 3 Trench Mortar Battery.

JULY 1916.

Army Form C. 2118.

V/3 T.M. By
1-31 July 1916

# WAR DIARY
## or
## INTELLIGENCE SUMMARY.
*(Erase heading not required.)*

Instructions regarding War Diaries and Intelligence Summaries are contained in F.S. Regs., Part II. and the Staff Manual respectively. Title pages will be prepared in manuscript.

| Place | Date | Hour | Summary of Events and Information | Remarks and references to Appendices |
|---|---|---|---|---|
| Audruicq | July 2/3 | 11 p.m. | Loading part of 3rd D.A.C. all night. Entrained in train 43 at 7 a.m. | |
| Boulogne | July 3 | 5 p.m. | arrived & detrained. unloaded train 43. | |
| Rouxtoux | July 4 | 7.30 a.m. | arrived by motor lorry. | |
| | | 6 p.m. | ordered to proceed to Daours, marching with 3rd D.A.C. | |
| Daours | July 5 | 7.30 a.m. | arrived Daours. | |
| Bois de Tailles | July 7 | | proceeded to a point W. of Bois de Tailles on Bray-Corbie Road. | |
| Bray | " 9 | | N. " Bray (about 1 mile) | |
| | " 10 | | attached to 23rd F.A. Bgde as working party; employed making dugouts and roads. | |
| | " 14 | | Capt R.S. Killed, appointed acting T.M.C. vice Capt R.S. Johnson 2nd Lt Spiers assumed provisional command | |
| | " 17 | | moved forward with 23rd Bgde to area S.21.d - 22.c to assist with gun pits &c. & in the attack. |
| | " 17 | 9.50 p.m. | Enemy put a very strong gas barrage across Montauban, until 4.30 a.m. 18th. | |
| | " 18 | | Enemy very active in this area all day. | |
| | " 19 | | Enemy continued heavy shelling. Moved back to Bray to reach billet | |
| | " 22 | | Received one 240 mm Morten from 16th division. | |
| | " 29 | | 25 men attached to 42nd Bgde as working party. Work much interrupted by shelling at A3a. | |
| | " 30 | | 25 men rejoined battery. | |

Lieut T. Hack
2nd Lt PRA
Comg V/3 T.M. T.M.B.

3rd Divisional Artillery.

V / 3 TRENCH MORTAR BATTERY.

A U G U S T   1 9 1 6.

Army Form C. 2118.

# WAR DIARY
## INTELLIGENCE SUMMARY
*(Erase heading not required).*

V/3 T.M. Battery

1 - 31st August

| Place | Date | Hour | Summary of Events and Information | Remarks and references to Appendices |
|---|---|---|---|---|
| BRAY | Aug 1. | | Moved to Rest area. Battery employed during rest at railhead ammunition dump | |
| DORNANCOURT | 2 | | " Battery employed as working parties to S.A. Brigades | |
| BRAY | 19 to 20 | | " Battery employed as working parties to S.A. Brigades | |
| | 20 | | Ordered to place one mortar in action against Guillemont. Finding this impossible in the time given, ordered to withdraw. | |
| TRONES WOOD | 21 /31 | | Ordered to start digging emplacement, in order to put one mortar into action against Guillemont. Continued working till the end of the month. The mortar was placed in position on the night of the 26/27 with 20 rounds of ammunition. During this period, one man wounded. | |

[signature] 2/Lt
R.F.A.
Cmdg. V/3 Hy. T.M. Battery

DIVISION AMMUNITION
COLUMN.
1914 AUG TO 1919 SEPT.
TRENCH MORTAR BTY'S
1915 JULY TO 1919 FEB

1402

3RD DIVISION
DIVL. ARTILLERY

TRENCH MORTAR BATTERIES.

~~1918~~

1918 JAN — 1919 FEB

January 1918

COPY

**WAR DIARY**
or
**INTELLIGENCE SUMMARY.**
(Erase heading not required.)

Army Form C. 2118.

From 1st to 31st January 1918

3rd Divl. L.M. Batteries

| Place | Date | Hour | Summary of Events and Information | Remarks and references to Appendices |
|---|---|---|---|---|
| MORY | 1st to 7th | | Batteries engaged in the BULLECOURT sector, in retaliatory firing, and harassing fire, also in repairing and strengthening existing positions. In the NORFUIL sector a site was found upon which satisfactory retaliatory firing on the first position was made on the two new bunk positions in MARTON TRENCH | |
| | 8th to 14th 31st | | Batteries in both sectors were engaged in firing on all lines in answer to a call. The Batteries in the BULLECOURT sector engaged in retaliatory firing, repairing on existing [?] to repairing and improving existing positions, and the construction of new [?]. In the NORFUIL sector, Batteries were engaged in retaliatory firing, and engaged in repairing and strengthening the existing position, and preparing for directly new positions. The two new burst positions in MARTON TRENCH. Before the guns were taken into action. Retaliatory firing has been carried from these new positions also a great deal of registration on special targets. The guns not in action were brought directly to [?] in the camp at MORY have been engaged in cleaning up the [?] and [?] and digging trenches [?] on [?]. making such improvements as against [?] [?] as the [?]. A considerable [?] improved during the above period, and the amount of ammunition expended is as follows:— About 554 rounds | |

(Sgd.) E.B. BACKHOUSE Capt.
for O.I.M.B.O. 3rd Divl. Arty.

# WAR DIARY or INTELLIGENCE SUMMARY

Army Form C. 2118.

January 1918

3rd Div. T.M. Batteries

(Erase heading not required.)

| Place | Date | Hour | Summary of Events and Information | Remarks and references to Appendices |
|---|---|---|---|---|
| MORY | 1st to 7th | | Batteries engaged in the BULLECOURT retaliatory firing answering S.O.S. calls, and generally employed in repairing and strengthening existing firing positions. In the NOREUIL sector little firing was done except occasional retaliatory answer and good progress was made on the two new trench positions in MALTON TRENCH. | |
| | 8th | | Batteries on both sectors were engaged in firing on S.O.S. lines in answer to a call, though our own attempts at said S.O.S. lines. | |
| | 9th to 31st | | The Batteries on the BULLECOURT sector retaliatory firing, registering on various targets repairing and improving existing positions, and the installing of winter positions. In the NOREUIL the Batteries were engaged in retaliation firing and engaging in repairing and strengthening and completing the two new positions in MALTON TRENCH, which were also in action. Retaliatory firing has been carried out from these new positions, also a good deal of registration on general targets. The men settling in dugouts in the camp at MORY were employed in digging out dugouts in an action and digging in an arrival at later, making and improving, and against hostile aeroplanes. No casualties have occurred during the entire time and ammunition expended is estimated at about 53% rounds. | |

A. E. ?? Major
O.C. 3rd Div. T.M. Batteries

Army Form C. 2118.

# WAR DIARY
or
## INTELLIGENCE SUMMARY.
(Erase heading not required.)

2nd Divisional T.M. Battery

February 1918

Instructions regarding War Diaries and Intelligence Summaries are contained in F.S. Regs., Part II. and the Staff Manual respectively. Title pages will be prepared in manuscript.

| Place | Date | Hour | Summary of Events and Information | Remarks and references to Appendices |
|---|---|---|---|---|
| MORY | 7th | | Heavy & medium batteries engaged on the BULLECOURT and NOREUIL sectors on retaliatory firing and improving and repairing gun positions. The heavies were engaged also on counter battery shoots in the NOREUIL sector. | |
| | 8th | | Relieved by 59th Div. T.M. Batteries on the BULLECOURT and NOREUIL sectors. Handed over 2 9.45in MK III guns, 2 2.48in MK I guns, and 12 Stokes mortar guns. | |
| | 8th | | Guns relieved were from old batteries proceeded to BOIRY BECQUERELLE and rebuilt the 2in, 12 Dec 17 Div 6 Corps area as the QUEMAPPE front. | |
| BOIRY BECQUERELLE | 9th | | Remainder of batteries proceeded to BOIRY BECQUERELLE and completed the handing over altogether 2 9.45in MK III, 2 9.45in MK I, and 16 2inch Stokes mortar guns. | |
| | 10th to 28th | | Medium batteries engaged during this period in machinery drills, reports to the existing gun positions held being dugouts and gun pits etc in an unserviceable condition and finally also in reconnaissance for new ones. The heavy batteries handed over similar shoots by gun and also engaged in similar reconnaissance and routine duties. The batteries during the entire period had a course of training in map reading, gas drills, etc... Ammunition and the amount of ammunition expended during the period — 1195 rounds in all. (9.45 q. 45" Frank T, and 16 rounds 2" T.M.R mortar T.M. | |

Signed M. G. A. Hay
O.C. 2nd Div. T.M. Battery

3rd Divisional Artillery.

--------

D. T. M. O.

3rd DIVISIONAL TRENCH MORTARS

MARCH 1918

Army Form C. 2118.

**WAR DIARY**
or
**INTELLIGENCE SUMMARY.**
(Erase heading not required.)

3rd Divisional T.M. Batteries  March 1918  Trench Mortar Batteries

From 1st to 31st March 1918

| Place | Date | Hour | Summary of Events and Information | Remarks and references to Appendices |
|---|---|---|---|---|
| BOIRY-BECQUERELLE | 1st to 5th | | Medium and heavy batteries engaged in retaliatory firing and wire cutting, repairing all existing gun positions, and building new positions for 6 inch T.Ms on the CHERISY front. | |
| | 6th | | Reorganisation of 9th Batteries. 2 Officers and 24 ORs transferred to new VI Corps Heavy Artillery, and 2. 9.45 inch Mark III T.Ms and 1 Mark I. also handed over, the remaining Officers and other ranks being absorbed by the two existing batteries, X & Y | |
| | 7th to 16th | | The two batteries were engaged in building and constructing new silk inch positions on the left sector, repair of existing positions, retaliatory firing, and wire cutting in preparation for raids by the infantry on the divisional front. | |
| | 20th | | | |
| | 21st | | Attack by the enemy. Both batteries firing on S.O.S lines, and three guns on the right sector destroyed, after all ammunition had been fired, owing to the partial evacuation of the front according to orders. | |
| | 22nd & 23rd | | Continuation of enemy attack. Batteries fired on S.O.S lines as long as possible, three guns being destroyed by us, and six buried before finial evacuation. Personnel in billet at BOIRY BECQUEREILE evacuated billet under orders and marched to NEUVILLE VITASSE afterwards proceeding to FICHEUX and joining the 3rd D.A.C. | |
| | 24th | | Batteries moved to BRETENCOURT, the personnel assisting the 3rd D.A.C in the ammunition dump on the BLAIREVILLE - BRETENCOURT road. | |
| | 25th to 29th | | Personnel engaged on the Ammunition dump with 3rd D.A.C another party of 20 being attached to H.Q. 46 R.F.A for one day, but not being required, worked on the removal of wounded. | |
| | 30th | | Marched to new billets at BAVINCOURT. | |
| | | | Ammunition expended during the above operations 6 inch 1917 rounds, 9.45" 1544 rounds. Casualties during month 3 ORanks wounded, 2 ORanks wounded (gas) and 1 ORank wounded remaining at duty. | |

D. McClure Captain
for O.C. 46 R.F.A 3rd Div

3rd Divisional Artillery

**WAR DIARY**

3rd DIVISIONAL TRENCH MORTAR OFFICER

APRIL 1918

Army Form C. 2118.

From 1st to 30th April 1918

3rd Div. T.M. Batteries

VBC 18

# WAR DIARY
## or
## INTELLIGENCE SUMMARY
(Erase heading not required.)

April 1918

Instructions regarding War Diaries and Intelligence Summaries are contained in F.S. Regs., Part II. and the Staff Manual respectively. Title pages will be prepared in manuscript.

| Place | Date | Hour | Summary of Events and Information | Remarks and references to Appendices |
|---|---|---|---|---|
| BAVINCOURT ANEVAL | 1st | | Batteries moved by motor lorries to DIEVAL | |
| | 2nd & 3rd | | Batteries employed overhauling and cleaning arms and equipment. Moved to fresh billets at RUITZ | |
| RUITZ | 4th | | Batteries employed in training, rifle and marching drill, etc. | |
| | 5th–10th | | | |
| | 11th | 6.2–10p | Batteries proceeded to billets on SAILLY LABOURSE – NOYELLES road, and took over 4 bunch T.M.s in GORRE sector from 11th I.D. | |
| NOYELLES | 12th | | Handed over 4 bunch T.M.s in GORRE sector to 114th I.D., and proceeded by lorries to L'ABBAYE near OBLINGHEM, receiving 6 bunch T.M.s from I.D. XIII Corps | |
| OBLINGHEM | 13th & 14th | | Moved to fresh billets in OBLINGHEM sector. Batteries employed putting fire guns in the LOCON sector | |
| | 15th | | Handed over the fire guns on the line to 50th D.A., and moved to fresh billets in VENDIN-LEZ-BETHUNE, where another gun area put in action on the LOCON sector, and 6 bunch T.M.s received from I.D. XIII Corps | |
| VENDIN-LEZ-BETHUNE | 16th to 21st | | Batteries employed making positions for 2 bunch T.M.s, and putting them in action, also strengthening existing positions | |
| | 22nd | | Moved to fresh billets in CHOCQUES | |
| CHOCQUES | 23rd | | Took over 4 bunch T.M.s and 1 – 9.45" MK III T.M. from 1st I.D. in the LOCON sector, and handed over 4 bunch T.M.s at billets to 4th I.D. | |
| | 22nd | | Batteries engaged repairing and strengthening all gun positions, and constructing dug outs in positions for gun detachments. Firing only in registration and remained stabilization | |
| | 29th | | | |
| | 30th | | Handed over 1 – 9.45" MK III T.M. to V/XIII H.J. T.M. Bty. | |
| | | | Ammunition expended during above period T.M.G. 60 rounds | |
| | | | Casualties 1 O.R. wounded. | |

C. Wills Captain
10 J. S. O. 3rd Div.

From 1st to 31st May 1918
Army Form C. 2118.

3rd Divisional S.A.A Positions

# WAR DIARY
## or
## INTELLIGENCE SUMMARY.
(Erase heading not required.)

| Place | Date | Hour | Summary of Events and Information | Remarks and references to Appendices |
|---|---|---|---|---|
| CHOQUES | 1st to 31st | | Both medium batteries were engaged during the month, in registering and engaging gun positions in both sectors of the Divisional Front. They were also engaged in the construction of new positions for back S.A.A. [illeg] ammunition recesses in all positions, and the building of dugouts for the gun detachments. For S.A.A was now in action. | |
| | | | 196 rounds have been fired in answer to S.O.S. calls. | |
| | | | Casualties during the month - 2 O.Rs killed, 4 O.Rs wounded, 1 O.R remained remaining at duty | |

[signature] Captain
O.C. A/3rd [?]

Army Form C. 2118.

From 1st to 30th June 1918

# WAR DIARY
## or
## INTELLIGENCE SUMMARY.
(Erase heading not required.)

3rd Div^t R.A. L.M. Batteries

Vol 20

| Place | Date | Hour | Summary of Events and Information | Remarks and references to Appendices |
|---|---|---|---|---|
| CHOCQUES | 1st to 13th | | Both medium batteries were engaged, on the LOCON and HINGES sectors, in the construction of dugouts on gun positions, and on repairing and strengthening emplacements, making alternative gun positions, and the building of ammunition recesses where they were necessary. | |
| | 14th to 15th | | Both batteries were engaged in conjunction with the artillery, in firing on special targets in support of the infantry, during operations carried out by the division, afterwards standing by to answer S.O.S. calls. | |
| | 16th to 30th | | Work was continued on emplacements and dugouts, during this period by the batteries, much work being done. Guns at all times being manned, to answer S.O.S. calls. | |
| | | | During the above period the following amount of ammunition was expended:— T.M.G. 2/3 rounds | |
| | | | The total casualties were:— 3 O. Ranks wounded. | |

4/1/8

[signature] Captain
I.O. T.M.O. 3rd Div

# WAR DIARY
## or
## INTELLIGENCE SUMMARY

3rd Divisional Trench Mortar Batteries. From 1st July to 31st July 1918

Army Form C. 2118.

| Place | Date | Hour | Summary of Events and Information | Remarks and references to Appendices |
|---|---|---|---|---|
| CHOCQUES | 1st to 31st | | Both batteries were engaged during the month, on the HINGES and LOCON sectors in the harassing of forward active positions, not the construction of ammunition recesses on the emplacements, and putting the guns in action, after which a serious amount of firing on different targets was carried out. Such work was done, on the repair of weary emplacements and trenches round positions, the strengthening of which was considered to be urgently needed, owing to the large amount of rain that had fallen, there repairs are still being carried out. Guns were at all times manned to answer S.O.S calls. The amount of ammunition expended during the month was 134 rounds T.M. Casualties to personnel Nil. | |

(signature)
Lieut Colonel
O.I.6. C. Batteries

**Army Form C. 2118.**

# WAR DIARY
## or
## INTELLIGENCE SUMMARY

(Erase heading not required.)

**3rd Div. T.M. Batteries**

**August 1918**

Sheet 1.

| Place | Date | Hour | Summary of Events and Information | Remarks and references to Appendices |
|---|---|---|---|---|
| CHOCQUES | 1st - 6th | | Batteries engaged in repairing and strengthening all existing gun positions, on the LOCON and HINGES sectors, and firing on special targets. Handed over 12 T.M.s in the line to 19th Div. T.M.B. taking over the same number from them at the billets, and moved by lorries to BAILLEUL-LES-PERNES. | |
| BAILLEUL-LES-PERNES | 8th - 12th | | Batteries engaged in training. Rifle and Revolver instruction, gun drill and gun laying, physical drill, signalling, etc. | |
| | 13th | | Moved by lorries to CANETTEMONT, with all guns and equipment. | |
| CANETTEMONT | 14th | | Moved to HUMBERCOURT by lorries. | |
| HUMBERCOURT | 15th - 19th | | Batteries engaged in training. Gun drill and gun laying, signalling, including laying out and maintenance of lines, instruction in morse code, etc. One officer and 50 O.Ranks proceeded to the ammunition dumps at POMMIER to work, the remainder being engaged in training, etc. | |
| " " | 20th | | Remainder of the T.M. personnel moved by lorry to POMMIER, leaving all guns at HUMBERCOURT under a guard. | |
| " " | 26th | | All T.M. personnel, with the exception of those working at the A.R.P. proceeded to AYETTE sector, and were engaged in salving ammunition. | |
| POMMIER | 27th | | Salving ammunition near DOUCHY. Both batteries engaged at A.R.P. and on salving ammunition. Total rounds expended during four six days 63. T.M.G. Casualties Nil. | |
| | 29th / 31st | | | |

9/19

[signature] Captain
10 J 96 O 3rd Div. T.M.

# WAR DIARY

D.T.M.O. 3rd Division

2nd Div. I. to Batteries

Army Form C. 2118.

From 1st September 1918
To 30th September 1918

## INTELLIGENCE SUMMARY

| Place | Date | Hour | Summary of Events and Information | Remarks and references to Appendices |
|---|---|---|---|---|
| | 1st, 2nd | | Batteries engaged at A.R.P. and salving ammunition. | |
| | 3rd | | Moved to hut camp near BOIRY ST RECTOR. | |
| | 4th, 5th | | Batteries engaged at A.R.P. and salving ammunition. | |
| | 6th | | Men and behaviour of personnel removed to camp near ST LEGER where T.M. personnel reported from A.R.P. on 7th inst. | |
| | 8th | | Moved to camp near ADINFER. | |
| | 9th, 11th | | Batteries engaged salving ammunition. | |
| | 12th | | Moved to camp near GOMIECOURT. | |
| | 13th | | Moved to camp at VAULX-VRAUCOURT where working parties were sent to A.R.P. at VELU. | |
| | 14th, 20th | | Batteries were engaged at A.R.P. and salving Enemy dumps. | |
| | 30th | | O.C. and personnel of personnel moved to VELU on 28th inst, camp at eastern HAVRINCOURT arrived on 29th inst, and camp north of HAVRINCOURT village on 30th. No casualties to officers or O. Ranks received during the month. | |

10/12/18

3rd Divisional Trench Mortar Batteries

**WAR DIARY**
or
**INTELLIGENCE SUMMARY**

Army Form C. 2118.

3rd Div. T.M. Batteries

From: 1st to 30 October 1918

Vol 24

| Place | Date | Hour | Summary of Events and Information | Remarks and references to Appendices |
|---|---|---|---|---|
| | 1st to 10th | | Batt. re-engaged as A.R.P. M.G. and division of personnel moved to camp near MASNIERES | |
| | 11th to 31st | | Batteries engaged as A.R.P. H.Q. and remainder of personnel moved to CATTENIERES on 18th inst. to QUIVY on 23rd instant, and to ROMERIES on 26th instant 1 OR wounded on 26th instant, remained at duty 1 OR wounded on 29th instant & admitted to Hospital | |

Captain
D.T.M.O. 3rd Div.

3rd Division
———————

Herewith War Diary for Nov. for 3rd Divisional Trench Mortars which was not available when the remainder were sent to you at the beginning of the month.

24.12.18.

W. L. [signature]
Capt. R.F.A.,
Brigade Major 3rd D.A.

Army Form C. 2118.

1st to 30th
NOVR. 1918.

# WAR DIARY
or
# INTELLIGENCE SUMMARY.
(Erase heading not required.)

3rd Div. Trench Mortar Batteries

VOL 25

Instructions regarding War Diaries and Intelligence Summaries are contained in F. S. Regs., Part II. and the Staff Manual respectively. Title pages will be prepared in manuscript.

| Place | Date | Hour | Summary of Events and Information | Remarks and references to Appendices |
|---|---|---|---|---|
| VERTAIN | 1st to 3rd | | Parties supplied for A.R.Ps from Lt. M. Batteries. All available personnel working on these working parties. | |
| | 4th 5th | | H.Q. and remainder of details removed to CAPELLE, and removed again on the 5th to VILLERS POL, the remainder still working on A.R.P. | |
| VILLERS POL | 9th | | H.Q. again removed to LE CHEVAL BLANC. Remainder of personnel working on dumps until 12th when they all rejoined their units. | |
| | 16th | | The whole of the T.M. personnel moved back to SOLESMES, billeted there one night, and proceeded to Third Army Reinforcement Camp CAMBRAI on the 17th. Leaving 3rd Div Reception Camp on the 18th, where the Batteries are still stationed. | |
| SOLESMES | 17th 18th 30th | | Batteries engaged in training, route marching, rifle drill, physical exercises, musketry, drill etc. Casualties 1 O.R. wounded. | |

(Sgd) ........... Captain
20 T.M.B.O. 3rd Div

Army Form C.2118.

# WAR DIARY
## or
## INTELLIGENCE SUMMARY.

(Erase heading not required.)

1st to 31st December 1918

December 1918    3rd Divisional. The Batteries

| Place | Date | Hour | Summary of Events and Information | Remarks and references to Appendices |
|---|---|---|---|---|
| | 1st to 26th | | Batteries billetted in SOLESMES. Officers and other ranks engaged in keeping self by means of drills, marching and physical exercises with exercises, route marches and general games and other sports. | |
| | 27th 28th | | Proceeded by rail to DÜREN and afterwards by Army Lorry to near 8 m N.E. to Wyn at LENDERSDORF | |
| | 30th | | Marched into billets in NIDEGGEN where the whole of the 7th Divisional Artillery situated. | |

[signature]
Captain
O.C. his O 3rd D.A.

1/9

Army Form C. 2118.

# WAR DIARY
## or
## INTELLIGENCE SUMMARY.

1st to 31st January 1919

3rd Div. French Mortar Batteries

January 1919 (Erase heading not required.)

Instructions regarding War Diaries and Intelligence Summaries are contained in F. S. Regs., Part II. and the Staff Manual respectively. Title pages will be prepared in manuscript.

| Place | Date | Hour | Summary of Events and Information | Remarks and references to Appendices |
|---|---|---|---|---|
| NIDEGGEN | 1st to 31st | | 1 N.C.O. and 3 men supplied each day for guard at 18. A.D.H.Q. Remainder of personnel engaged during the month in private mounted foot-drill, rifle drill, Physical drill, &c. Inspection and sport was also taken part in. Football matches six-a-side football tournaments, and whist drives and concerts | |

1-1-19

Ainsworth
Captain
O.3rd M.O. 3rd Div

WAR DIARY
or
INTELLIGENCE SUMMARY.

Army Form C. 2118.

(Erase heading not required.)

February 1919   3rd No. Seven Mortar Batteries

Instructions regarding War Diaries and Intelligence Summaries are contained in F.S. Regs., Part II. and the Staff Manual respectively. Title pages will be prepared in manuscript.

| Place | Date | Hour | Summary of Events and Information | Remarks and references to Appendices |
|---|---|---|---|---|
| NIDEGGEN | 1st to 28th | | 1 NCO + 3 men supplied each day for guard at RAHQ. Remainder of Personnel engaged during the month in route marches, foot drill, Rifle Exercises & Recreation and sport. Was also taken part in football matches on a side of a tournament which drew some concerts. | |

(Signed)
Captain
OC 3rd No. Seven Mortar Battery

NORTHERN DIVISION
(LATE 3RD DIVISION)

3RD DIVL AMMN COLN.

JAN - SEP 1919

NORTHERN DIVISION
(LATE 3RD DIVISION)

1st to 31st January 1919

Army Form C. 2118.

3rd D.A.C.

Vol 4.8

# WAR DIARY
or
## INTELLIGENCE SUMMARY.

(Erase heading not required.)

Instructions regarding War Diaries and Intelligence Summaries are contained in F. S. Regs., Part II. and the Staff Manual respectively. Title pages will be prepared in manuscript.

| Place | Date | Hour | Summary of Events and Information | Remarks and references to Appendices |
|---|---|---|---|---|
| LENDERSDORP (GERMANY) | Jan 1st 1919 – Jan 31st 1919 | | No change. | |

Army Form C. 2118.

# WAR DIARY
## or
## INTELLIGENCE SUMMARY.

3rd D.A.C.

(Erase heading not required.)

| Place | Date | Hour | Summary of Events and Information | Remarks and references to Appendices |
|---|---|---|---|---|
| LENDERSDORF | Feb 1st 25A | | No change | 98649 hrs |

J.S. Brown
Lieut Col.
O.C. 3rd D.A.C.

<u>Confidential</u>

<u>War Diary</u>

of

<u>Northern Divisional Ammunition Column</u>

From 1st March 1919    To 31st March 1919

(Volume 43.)

# WAR DIARY
## or
## INTELLIGENCE SUMMARY.
*(Erase heading not required.)*

Army Form C. 2118.

| Place | Date | Hour | Summary of Events and Information | Remarks and references to Appendices |
|---|---|---|---|---|
| BRAUWEILER. | 14/3/19 | | Coehan of unit :-  HEADQUARTERS. & No 1 SECTION. BRAUWEILER. No 2 SECTION. WIDDERSDORF. S.A.A. SECTION. BUSCHBELL. | |
| | 14/3/19 | | 1 Riders 3 L Stants and 5 Mules category D.X. sent to Abatteir COLOGNE for destruction. | |
| | 14/3/19 | | G.O.C. 3rd DIVISION inspected S.A.A. SECTION at BUSCHBELL. 6 Riders 3 L Stants of "Y" category sent to KREUZAN (S. of DUREN) and rechanged with 3rd D.A.C. for 6 corresponding number "X" category animals. 1 Rider 3 L. Horse & 5 mules received from 3rd D.A.C. in place of a corresponding number sent to COLOGNE on 14/3/19 for destruction. | |
| | | | COLONEL C. B. WATKINS. C.B. Lieut P.A. CAMPSIE Lieut E.S.L. TINNEY and Lieut J. I. WILLIAMS with 15 O.R. from D.A.C. started for London for TRIUMPHAL MARCH PAST of the GUARDS. | |

Army Form C. 2118.

# WAR DIARY
## or
## INTELLIGENCE SUMMARY.
(Erase heading not required.)

Instructions regarding War Diaries and Intelligence Summaries are contained in F. S. Regs., Part II. and the Staff Manual respectively. Title pages will be prepared in manuscript.

| Place | Date | Hour | Summary of Events and Information | Remarks and references to Appendices |
|---|---|---|---|---|
| BRAUWEILER | 18/3/19 | | G.O.C. 3rd DIVISION inspected Headquarters and No.1 SECTION at BRAUWEILER, and No.2 SECTION at WIDDERSDORF. He was very pleased with all he saw. | |
| | 20/3/19 | | Lieut (a/Captain) R.O. COOKE taken from No.2 Brigade S.S.S. to No 1 SECTION. | |
| | 25/3/19 | | S.A.A. SECTION moved from BRAUWEILER from BUSCHBELL to SINTHERN. | |
| | 27/3/19 | | The following Officers having joined from Base are posted to echelon as shown:- Lieut F.J. LAST. No.1 SECTION. " H.H. STONE. No.2 SECTION. " A.C.P. BRIGGS. S.A.A. SECTION. | |
| | | | A party of 9 O.R. transferred to the 2nd D.A.C. preparatory to going home for demobilization. A draft of 51 O.R. were received from 2nd Echelon in exchange. | |
| | | | 10. O.R. left for England for demobilization. | |

Army Form C. 2118.

# WAR DIARY
## or
## INTELLIGENCE SUMMARY.

(Erase heading not required.)

| Place | Date | Hour | Summary of Events and Information | Remarks and references to Appendices |
|---|---|---|---|---|
| BRAUWEILER | 28/3/19 | | The GUARDS STRING BAND gave a performance to the B.A.C. at 1400 hours. | |
| | | | Lieut T.J. DARLISTON having found from Base to proceed to S.A.A. SECTION. | |
| | | | 8 O.R. proceeded to England for demobilization. | |
| | 29/3/19 | | Lieut H.H STOWE (No2 SECTION) posted to No1. B.A.C. 3 O.R. proceeded to England for demobilization. | |
| | 30/3/19. | | The following Officers having joined from 155 R.G. Brigade R.F.A. are attached to Sections as shown. | |
| | | | Lieut W.H. LLEWELLYN.   No 2 SECTION | |
| | | | " W. H. CALVERT.   S.A.A. SECTION. | |
| | 31/3/19 | | 6 O.R. proceeded to England for demobilization | |

Army Form C. 2118.

# WAR DIARY
## or
## INTELLIGENCE SUMMARY.
(Erase heading not required.)

| Place | Date | Hour | Summary of Events and Information | Remarks and references to Appendices |
|---|---|---|---|---|
| | | | SUMMARY. | |
| | | | | OFF O.R. |
| | | | Admitted to hospital — 10 |
| | | | Discharged from hospital — 6 |
| | | | Evacuated to C.C.S. — 11 |
| | | | Returned from Evacuation — 2 |
| | | | Reinforcements received — 133 |
| | | | Transfer from 3rd R.Bn — 52 |
| | | | To England for demobilization — 34 |
| | | | Re-enlistments under A.O. 6/IV. — 0 |
| | | | Proceeded on Leave to U.K. 5 0 |
| | | | |
| | | | Amount of Sm. Ammunition Received Rounds "2" |
| | | | Amount of Sm. Ammunition Issued " "3" |
| | | | |
| | | | WynnThomas Colonel 6.9.19 |
| | | | Commanding Northn. T.C. |

Instructions regarding War Diaries and Intelligence Summaries are contained in F. S. Regs., Part II. and the Staff Manual respectively. Title pages will be prepared in manuscript.

Appendix "A."

Northern Divisional Ammunition Column.

Statement of Ammunition Received during month of March.

2391 rounds "A.X." fuze 106.
786 rounds "A." fuze 80.
80 rounds "A.X." fuze 101 delay action.
451. rounds "B.X." fuze 101 non-delay action.

Colonel.C.B., R.A.
1st April 1919. Commanding Northern Divisional Ammn. Col.

Appendix.

## Northern Divisional Ammunition Column.

Statement of Ammunition Issued during month of March.

| | |
|---|---|
| 74th Brigade., R.F.A. | 262 rds "A.X." fuze 106. |
| 75th Brigade., R.F.A. | 485 "A.X." fuze 106. |
| 75th Brigade., R.F.A. | 503 rds. "A." fuze 80. |
| 75th Brigade., R.F.A. | 65 rds. "B.X." fuze 101. |

Colonel., C.B., R.A.

1st April 1919.   Commanding Northern Divisional Ammn. Col.

Army Form C. 2118.

# WAR DIARY
## or
## INTELLIGENCE SUMMARY.

North 2 Aux Col

(Erase heading not required.)

Instructions regarding War Diaries and Intelligence Summaries are contained in F. S. Regs., Part II. and the Staff Manual respectively. Title pages will be prepared in manuscript.

| Place | Date | Hour | Summary of Events and Information | Remarks and references to Appendices |
|---|---|---|---|---|
| | 1/4/19 | | Position of Unit :- | |
| | | | HEADQUARTERS & NO. 1. SECTION - BRAUWEILER 8.MILES. WEST of COLOGNE. | |
| | | | NO. 2 SECTION. - WIDDERSDORF. 6 " " " | |
| | | | S.A.A. SECTION. - SINTHERN. | |
| BRAUWEILER | 1/4/19 | | 88 H.D. Horses sent to Animal Collecting Camp COLOGNE and 151 Mules received. | |
| | 2/4/19 | | 4 H.D. Horses and 14 H.D. Mules sent to Abbatoir COLOGNE 59 Other Ranks posted from 2nd Army R.A. Reinforcement Camp COLOGNE. | |

Army Form C. 2118.

# WAR DIARY
*or*
# INTELLIGENCE SUMMARY.
*(Erase heading not required.)*

Instructions regarding War Diaries and Intelligence Summaries are contained in F. S. Regs., Part II. and the Staff Manual respectively. Title pages will be prepared in manuscript.

| Place | Date | Hour | Summary of Events and Information | Remarks and references to Appendices |
|---|---|---|---|---|
| BRAUWEILER | 3/4/19 | | 2nd Lieut. C.T. CRAFER joined for duty and posted to S.A.A. Section. | |
| | 4/4/19 | | 10 Riding Horses received from Command Gathering Group. | |
| | | | COLOGNE. | |
| | | | 7 Other Ranks proceeded to England for demobilization. | |
| | 6/4/19 | | Major A. MacGregor RITCHIE. R.F.A. joined for duty. | |
| | | | 16 H. B.A.C. | |
| | 7/4/19 | | 2nd Lieut. L. DENISON proceeded to England for demobilization. | |

Army Form C. 2118.

# WAR DIARY
or
## INTELLIGENCE SUMMARY.
(Erase heading not required.)

Instructions regarding War Diaries and Intelligence Summaries are contained in F. S. Regs., Part II. and the Staff Manual respectively. Title pages will be prepared in manuscript.

| Place | Date | Hour | Summary of Events and Information | Remarks and references to Appendices |
|---|---|---|---|---|
| BRAUWEILER | 8/4/19 | | Major A. Macgregor RITCHIE. R.F.A. took over command of Northern Divisional Ammunition Column from Colonel C.B. WATKINS. C.B. 2nd Lieut. J.H. WHITE. joined for duty from 315 Bde. R.F.A. and posted to S.A.A SECTION. | |
| | 9/4/19 | | Colonel C.B WATKINS. C.B and 60. Other Ranks proceeded to ENGLAND. for Demobilization. | |
| | 11/4/19 | | 2nd Lieut. C.T. CRAFER and 71. Other Ranks proceeded to ENGLAND for Demobilization. | |
| | 12/4/19 | | Lecture given by PROFESSOR. ADKINS. at BRAUWEILER on the "BALKAN TRIANGLE". | |

Army Form C. 2118.

# WAR DIARY
## or
## INTELLIGENCE SUMMARY.

(Erase heading not required.)

Instructions regarding War Diaries and Intelligence Summaries are contained in F. S. Regs., Part II. and the Staff Manual respectively. Title pages will be prepared in manuscript.

| Place | Date | Hour | Summary of Events and Information | Remarks and references to Appendices |
|---|---|---|---|---|
| BRAUWEILER | 12/4/19 | | (Contd.) 23 Riding and 82 Mules Classified "Z" sent to Armored Collecting Camp COLOGNE. | |
| | 13/4/19 | | Lieut. SIR MARKHAM joined for duty from 3rd DIV. AMM. COL. and posted to HEADQUARTERS as Educational Officer. | |
| | | | Lieut. H.B. REID, joined for duty from 3rd DIV. AMM COL. and posted to No. 2. SECTION. | |
| | | | Lieut J.E. JACKSON, joined for duty from 17th DIVISION and posted to No. 1. SECTION. | |
| | | | Captain G.W. WESTON, joined from 3rd DIV AMM COL. and took over command of No. 1 SECTION. | |
| | | | Lieut. H.G. ANSELL, joined for duty from 17th DIVISION with M.T. and posted to S.A.A. SECTION. | |
| | 14/4/19 | | 2nd Lieut. J.R. DARLING, joined for duty from 17th DIVISION and posted to No. 2. SECTION. | |

**Army Form C. 2118.**

# WAR DIARY
or
## INTELLIGENCE SUMMARY.
(Erase heading not required.)

Instructions regarding War Diaries and Intelligence Summaries are contained in F.S. Regs., Part II. and the Staff Manual respectively. Title pages will be prepared in manuscript.

| Place | Date | Hour | Summary of Events and Information | Remarks and references to Appendices |
|---|---|---|---|---|
| BRAUWEILER | 18/4/19 | | Lieut. G. GORDON. joined for duty from 3rd DIV. AMM. COL. and posted to No. 1. SECTION. Lieut. G.F. GUSH. joined for duty from 33rd DIVISION and posted to No. 2. SECTION. | |
| | 19/4/19 | | 18. Riding Horses received from 75th Bde. R.F.A. | |
| | 19/4/19 | | 33. Mules Classified "Z" sent to Animal Collecting Camp COLOGNE. | |
| | 21/4/19 | | 2. L.D. Horses and 9. Riding sent to Animal Collecting Camp COLOGNE. Lieut. A.C. BALL. MC. R.G.A. joined for duty and posted to No. 2. SECTION. Parties from D.A.C. proceeded by Lorry to a Lecture given at LOVENICH by the REVD. CANON J.J. PARFIT. on "BAGHDAD THE PLOT THAT FAILED". The C.R.A. NORTHERN DIVISION inspected Unit Registers at LOVENICH. | |
| | 22/4/19 | | | |

Army Form C. 2118.

# WAR DIARY
or
# INTELLIGENCE SUMMARY.

(Erase heading not required.)

Instructions regarding War Diaries and Intelligence Summaries are contained in F. S. Regs., Part II. and the Staff Manual respectively. Title pages will be prepared in manuscript.

| Place | Date | Hour | Summary of Events and Information | Remarks and references to Appendices |
|---|---|---|---|---|
| BRAUWEILER | 24/4/19 | | Parties from D.A.C. proceeded by lorry to a lecture given on KLEIN KONIGSDORF by Commander VISCOUNT BROOME R.N. on Naval Subjects illustrated by slides. | |
| | 26/4/19 | | 5. Rising sent to amused Collecting Camp COLOGNE. Lieut. W.H. Llewellyn posted to MIDLAND DIVISION. | |
| | 24/4/19 | | The G.O.C. NORTHERN DIVISION visited the D.A.C. HEADQUARTERS accompanied by the C.R.A. | |

Army Form C. 2118.

# WAR DIARY
## or
## INTELLIGENCE SUMMARY.
(Erase heading not required.)

| Place | Date | Hour | Summary of Events and Information | Remarks and references to Appendices |
|---|---|---|---|---|
| | | | SUMMARY.        Officers   O.R. | |
| | | | Admitted to Hospital.     4.    5. | |
| | | | Discharged from Hospital.    1.    2. | |
| | | | Evacuated to C.C.S. from Hospital.    -    3. | |
| | | | Rejoined from Evacuation.    -    1. | |
| | | | Proceeded to U.K. on Leave.    7.    67. | |
| | | | Proceeded to England for Demobilization.    5.    150. | |
| | | | Demobilized while on Leave in U.K.    -    1. | |
| | | | Arrangements made to dispose Services. | |

A.W. Ritchie
Major, R.F.A.
Commanding Northern 1912.C.

# WAR DIARY
## or
## INTELLIGENCE SUMMARY.
(Erase heading not required.)

Army Form C. 2118.

N.D.A.C

| Place | Date | Hour | Summary of Events and Information | Remarks and references to Appendices |
|---|---|---|---|---|
| | 1/5/19 | | Position of Unit:— | |
| | | | HEADQUARTERS & No. 1. SECTION - BRAUWEILER - 8 MILES WEST OF COLOGNE | |
| | | | No 2. SECTION — WIDDERSDORF 6 " | |
| | | | No 3. SECTION — SINTHERN 8 " | |
| BRAUWEILER | 1/5/19 | | LIEUT. P.G. McNINN Proceeded to ENGLAND for Demobilization. | |
| | | | The Commanding Officer lectured on "THE ZULU NATION" and the "ZULU REBELLION OF 1906" | |
| | 2/5/19 | | LIEUT. J.H. WHITE Proceeded to ENGLAND as unit Conducting Officer | |
| | | | 16 OR INDIAN Personnel proceeded to COLOGNE in charge of | |
| | | | Y.M.C.A. who provided refreshments and then were entrained | |
| | | | at Köln Nord for a trip to ? | |

Army Form C. 2118.

# WAR DIARY
## or
## INTELLIGENCE SUMMARY.
(Erase heading not required.)

| Place | Date | Hour | Summary of Events and Information | Remarks and references to Appendices |
|---|---|---|---|---|
| BRAUWEILER | 5/5/19 | | Commanding Officer inspected S.A.A. SECTION. | |
| " | 6/5/19 | | Commanding Officer inspected No. 2. SECTION. | |
| " | 9/5/19 | | The Commanding Officer with Officers for Section and 19 O.R. BRITISH & INDIAN attended the NORTHERN DIVISIONAL Review held by H.R.H. the Duke of Connaught. | |
| " | 10/5/19 | | Ladies Concert Party visited the D.A.C. and rendered a very successful programme which was much appreciated by all Ranks. | |
| " | 12/5/19 | | 13 pairs of wheelers were furnished to move the Royal Scots to MULHEIM. | |
| " | 14/5/19 | | Party of INDIAN O.R. proceeded to COLOGNE Guests as a feed being provided by the Y.M.C.A. | |

Army Form C. 2118.

# WAR DIARY
## or
## INTELLIGENCE SUMMARY.
*(Erase heading not required.)*

Instructions regarding War Diaries and Intelligence Summaries are contained in F. S. Regs., Part II. and the Staff Manual respectively. Title pages will be prepared in manuscript.

| Place | Date | Hour | Summary of Events and Information | Remarks and references to Appendices |
|---|---|---|---|---|
| Brookwood Camp | | | Draft of one Sergeant, one Bombardier & three Gunner Reinforcements went for Gunners duties from RA Reinforcement | |
| | 17/5/19 | | Draft of One Bombardier and twenty six Gunners and one NCO and Gunners Camp | |
| | 19/5/19 | | German Shoeing Smiths requisitioned for work in the SECTIONS | |
| | | | Three INDIAN O.R. proceeded on leave to YMCA College on 10 days | |
| | 21/5/19 | | Two 18 pounder Guns received from LIGHT DIVISION gun Limbers for 6 Inch Howitzers | |
| | 24/5/19 | | One Lance Naik and two OR INDIAN returned from leave | |
| | 29/5/19 | | Surplus Ammunition (owing to 4 Gun Establishment) returned to Railhead | |
| | | | Draft of 1 Sheeting Smith returned from 10 days leave | |

Army Form C. 2118.

# WAR DIARY
or
# INTELLIGENCE SUMMARY.

(Erase heading not required.)

Instructions regarding War Diaries and Intelligence Summaries are contained in F. S. Regs., Part II. and the Staff Manual respectively. Title pages will be prepared in manuscript.

| Place | Date | Hour | Summary of Events and Information | Remarks and references to Appendices |
|---|---|---|---|---|
| BRAUWEILER | 30/5/19 | | LIEUT. A.O.R BRIGGS proceeded to NEWMARKET ENGLAND on Educational Course. | |
| | | | Equipment Surplus to A Gun Establishment handed in by ctos 1 and 2. SECTIONS. | |
| " | 31/5/19 | | "THE NORTHERN LIGHTS" Concert Party gave an excellent concert in the theatre BRAUWEILER | |

Army Form C. 2118.

# WAR DIARY
## or
## INTELLIGENCE SUMMARY.
(Erase heading not required.)

Instructions regarding War Diaries and Intelligence Summaries are contained in F. S. Regs., Part II. and the Staff Manual respectively. Title pages will be prepared in manuscript.

| Place | Date | Hour | Summary of Events and Information | Remarks and references to Appendices |
|---|---|---|---|---|
| | | | SUMMARY. | |
| | | | Admitted to Hospital. Officers — O.R. 13. | |
| | | | Discharged from Hospital. — 4 | |
| | | | Evacuated to C.C.S. from Hospital. — - | |
| | | | Rejoined from Evacuation. — - | |
| | | | Proceeded to U.K. on leave. 4 80. | |
| | | | Proceeded to England for Demobilization. 1 4 | |
| | | | Demobilized while on leave in U.K. — - | |
| | | | Re-Enlisted for one year. — 2 | |

[signature]
MAJOR R. F. A.
COMMANDING NORTHERN DIVL. AMM. COL.

Army Form C. 2118.

Northern R&C

# WAR DIARY
## or
## INTELLIGENCE SUMMARY.
*(Erase heading not required.)*

Instructions regarding War Diaries and Intelligence Summaries are contained in F. S. Regs., Part II. and the Staff Manual respectively. Title pages will be prepared in manuscript.

| Place | Date | Hour | Summary of Events and Information | Remarks and references to Appendices |
|---|---|---|---|---|
| | | | Location of Unit. | |
| | | | Headquarters. 1.0.1.2. (BRAUWEILER) Sheet. I.L. | |
| | | | No 1. Section. 1.0.1.2. — " — GERMANY. | |
| | | | No 2. Section. 1.0.8.4. (WIDDERSDORF) | |
| | | | No 3. Section. 1.0.1.5. (SINTHERN) | |
| BRAUWEILER, GERMANY. | JUNE. 1919. | | | |
| | 3rd | | His Majesty's Birthday. Observed as a General Holiday. | |
| | 4th | | 11 Drivers joined from R.A. Reinforcement Camp. | |
| | 19th | | Marched to BRUCK-RATH Area bivouacing for night. | |
| | 20th | | Marched to IMMEKEPPEL-OBERSTEEG Area into bivouacs. | |
| | 30th | | Returned to BRUCK-RATH Area. | |

Instructions regarding War Diaries and Intelligence Summaries are contained in F. S. Regs., Part II. and the Staff Manual respectively. Title pages will be prepared in manuscript.

# WAR DIARY
*or*
# INTELLIGENCE SUMMARY.

*(Erase heading not required.)*

Army Form C. 2118.

| Place | Date | Hour | Summary of Events and Information | Remarks and references to Appendices |
|---|---|---|---|---|
| BRAUWEILER GERMANY | | | SUMMARY — JUNE. | |
| | | | PERSONNEL — Offs. O.R. | |
| | | | Granted Leave to U.K. 3. 15. | |
| | | | Demobilized: 1. Nil. | |
| | | | Admitted to Hospital. Nil 8 | |
| | | | Rejoined from Hospital. Nil 14 | |
| | | | Evacuated to C.C.S. Nil 5 | |
| | | | Reinforcements Joined. Nil 11 | |
| | | | ANIMALS | |
| | | | Evacuated to M.V.S. [illegible] | |

D. D. & L., London, E.C.
(A8004) Wt. W1771/M2 31 750,000 5/17 Sch. 52 Forms/C2118/14

Army Form C. 2118.

Instructions regarding War Diaries and Intelligence Summaries are contained in F.S. Regs., Part II. and the Staff Manual respectively. Title pages will be prepared in manuscript.

# WAR DIARY
## or
## INTELLIGENCE SUMMARY.
(Erase heading not required.)

Northern Dio[?]

| Place | Date | Hour | Summary of Events and Information | Remarks and references to Appendices |
|---|---|---|---|---|
| | July 1919. | | Location of Unit:— | |
| | | | Headquarters 1 - 0 - 2 (Brauweiler) Shut. I L. | |
| | | | No.1 Section 1 - 0 - 2 — do — Germany | |
| | | | No.2 Section 1 - 0 - 8 (Widdersdorf) | |
| | | | No.3 Section 1 - 0 - 5 (Sinthern) | |
| Brauweiler Germany. | 1st | | Marched from Rath back to old billets at Brauweiler, Sinthern & Widdersdorf. | |
| | 17th | | 69 Mules dispatched to White City, Cologne. | |
| | 18th | | Classification of 120 mules at Königsdorf | |
| | 20th | | 77 Mules classified "S" dispatched to White City, Cologne. | |
| | 26th | | Draft of 62 mules posted to D.A.C. | |
| | 31st | | D.A.C. moved transport of 76th B.A.C. from Mungersdorf to Mulheim Statn. | |

Army Form C. 2118.

# WAR DIARY
## or
## INTELLIGENCE SUMMARY.
(Erase heading not required.)

Instructions regarding War Diaries and Intelligence Summaries are contained in F. S. Regs., Part II. and the Staff Manual respectively. Title pages will be prepared in manuscript.

| Place | Date | Hour | Summary of Events and Information | Remarks and references to Appendices |
|---|---|---|---|---|

BRAUWEILER
GERMANY.

SUMMARY — JULY

PERSONNEL.  Offrs  OR.          ANIMALS.
Granted Leave to UK.   6.   57.       For sale. 146. Mules.
Demobilised.           2.    7.
Admitted to Hospital. Nil.  13.
Rejoined from Hospital. Nil.  6.
Evacuated to CCS.    Nil.   Nil.
Reinforcements Posted.  Nil.  62. (Indians)
* Posted to Home Establishment.

W. Bates. Capt.
Commanding [illegible] Remount [illegible]

# WAR DIARY or INTELLIGENCE SUMMARY

Army Form C. 2118.

*(Erase heading not required.)*

Northern J.C.

Instructions regarding War Diaries and Intelligence Summaries are contained in F.S. Regs., Part II. and the Staff Manual respectively. Title pages will be prepared in manuscript.

| Place | Date | Hour | Summary of Events and Information | Remarks and references to Appendices |
|---|---|---|---|---|
| Torgau nr Germany | August 1919 | | Location of Unit— | |
| | | | Headquarters 1 O. 1 N.C. (Bronsches) Shot 1 in Germany | |
| | | | 7/11 Scott 1 " 1 " " | |
| | | | 3rd C. Scott 1 " 1 O. 1 " (Wooderford?) | |
| | | | 7/3 Scotts 1 " 1 O. 1 " (Southern) | |
| | 3rd | | Escort for O.R. N.C. went to train met 6th N.C. ambulance & entrained | |
| | 5th | | 75 "S" Series inoculated & White Cell Count | |
| | 6th | | Draft of 11 Other Ranks R.A.M.C. | |
| | 7th | | Manifestos of the remnants of "B" Standard | |
| | 8th | | all 9 remnants Montreal | |
| | 10th | | Remnants Montreal | |

Army Form C. 2118.

# WAR DIARY
## or
## INTELLIGENCE SUMMARY.
*(Erase heading not required.)*

Instructions regarding War Diaries and Intelligence Summaries are contained in F. S. Regs., Part II. and the Staff Manual respectively. Title pages will be prepared in manuscript.

| Place | Date | Hour | Summary of Events and Information | Remarks and references to Appendices |
|---|---|---|---|---|
| Beaumetz Besnard | | | Summary for [illegible] | |
| | | | Personnel | |
| | | | Casualties to O.R. | |
| | | | Reinforcements | |
| | | | Casualties to horses | |
| | | | Reinforcements horses | |
| | | | Remounts & O.C.S. [illegible] | |
| | | | Recreation & sport | |
| | | | [illegible] | |

Army Form C. 2118.

# WAR DIARY
## or
## INTELLIGENCE SUMMARY.
(Erase heading not required.)

Northern 7 A C

Instructions regarding War Diaries and Intelligence Summaries are contained in F. S. Regs., Part II. and the Staff Manual respectively. Title pages will be prepared in manuscript.

| Place | Date | Hour | Summary of Events and Information | Remarks and references to Appendices |
|---|---|---|---|---|
| | | | Location of Unit | |
| | | | Headquarters 1.0.1.2 (BRAUWEILER) Sheet 14 GERMANY | |
| | | | No 1 Section 1.0.1.2 -Do- | |
| | | | No 2 Section 1.0.8.4 (WIDDERSDORF) -Do- | |
| | | | No 3 Section 1.0.1.5 (SINTHERN) | |
| September 1919 | | | | |
| Brauweiler Germany | 29.9.19 | | 30 hours carry on. Inspection by O.C. LAA Group arrived | |
| | | | early. While O.C. Cologne | |
| | 30.9.19 | | No 2 Transport Complete & despatched to O.C. H Corps Cologne | |
| | | | Lorries to Air City Cologne | |
| | 31.9.19 | | 31 Heavy Lorries Scam repair from H Corps HQ | |
| | 15.9.19 | | 1 Horse van & 1 cycle to H Motor Delivery Service | |

Army Form C. 2118.

# WAR DIARY
## or
## INTELLIGENCE SUMMARY.

*(Erase heading not required.)*

Instructions regarding War Diaries and Intelligence Summaries are contained in F. S. Regs., Part II. and the Staff Manual respectively. Title pages will be prepared in manuscript.

| Place | Date | Hour | Summary of Events and Information | Remarks and references to Appendices |
|---|---|---|---|---|
| BRUNELLA | 1-7-17 | | Instructions received from the Battle Headquarters System | |
| | 2-7-17 | | The E.R.A. Northern Division inspected the 200 C.B. | |
| | 3-7-17 | | 150 A.C.Cs. handed in dispatches to L Corps Command | |
| | | | Gallesburg Camp | |
| | 4-7-17 | | 21 Horses brought in dispatches to L Corps Command | |
| | | | Gallesburg Camp | |

Army Form C. 2118.

# WAR DIARY
## or
## INTELLIGENCE SUMMARY.

(Erase heading not required.)

Summary of Events and Information

| Place | Date | Hour | | Remarks and references to Appendices |
|---|---|---|---|---|
| BONNEHOEK GERMANY | | | SUMMARY September | |
| | | | | |
| | | | OFFICERS O.R. | |
| | | | Present | |
| | | | Casualties known to date  3   25 | |
| | | | Demobilized            2   20 | |
| | | | Admitted to Hospital   1    5 | |
| | | | Rejoined from Hospital 1    2 | |
| | | | Evacuated to CCS (wounded)  -   1 | |
| | | | Reinforcements Posted   Nil  Nil | |

AWRoberts
c/Lt Col R.F.A.
Commanding Northern D.A.C.

3rd Division

War Diaries

3/ Div. T. M. Battery.

1917 January to December

Army Form C. 2118.

# WAR DIARY or INTELLIGENCE SUMMARY

(Erase heading not required.)

Medium and Heavy Trench Mortars
3rd Div.
1st to 31st Jan, 1917.

Vol 3

Instructions regarding War Diaries and Intelligence Summaries are contained in F. S. Regs., Part II. and the Staff Manual respectively. Title Pages will be prepared in manuscript.

| Place | Date | Hour | Summary of Events and Information | Remarks and references to Appendices |
|---|---|---|---|---|
| BUS-EN ARTOIS | 10th to 31st Jany | | All Batteries were employed in making new gun positions and trenches at HEBUTERNE. On 1-1-17 2/Lt H.V.C. SUTHERLAND 2/3TMB was admitted to hospital. Lieut R.J. KITTEN R.F.A assumed command of X/3 T.M.Bty. Lt E.C. SNAPE returned from leave to UK on 2/1/17. 2/Lt C.A. WHITTAKER R.F.A returned from leave to UK on 4.1.17. Capt E.A. BACKHOUSE V/3 - Lt R.M.A Kent J/3 attended a course of Instruction at the enemy T.M School from 5-1-17 to 19-1-17. | |
| STOVEN | 15th to 28th/1/17 | | All Batteries moved to training area, where work at Thyaene during manoeuvring, saluting, two drill-arms series, out in accordance with 3F.A Training Programme. | |
| | 29th | | X/3 left for a course of instruction at S/S TM school on 23-1-16 | |
| | 30th | | Batteries moved to SARTON | |
| ROUBERS-SUR-OUCHE | 30th | | Batteries moved to ROUBERS-SUR-OUCHE. Jaqueleur Camp. | |

Chiswick Lt Col
R.F.A
Comdg. 3rd Div Medium
and Heavy Trench
Mortars F.A.

# WAR DIARY or INTELLIGENCE SUMMARY

Army Form C. 2118.

TRENCH MORTARS
31st Division
1st - 28th Feb 1917

Vol 8

| Place | Date | Hour | Summary of Events and Information | Remarks and references to Appendices |
|---|---|---|---|---|
| BUS LES ARTOIS / BERTRANCOURT | 1-2-17 | | 31st Divisional Trench mortar Batteries moved to ROUGECOURT-EN-L'EAU. | |
| | 2-2-17 to 7-2-17 | | Training carried out in accordance with Infantry training. On 5/2/17 Lt Col SNAPE R.F.A. O.C. X/3 gave a course of instruction at 31st Army Trench mortar School. | |
| | 8-2-17 | | Orders received to REGNEAUVILLETTE. | |
| | 9-2-17 to 17-2-17 | | Training on above continued. | |
| | | | Lieut REX O.N., under IL. at FATEM R.F.A. and 2nd Lt ...... to ARRAS, together with 2 Runners a ... from BUCQUOY attd[?] ... into BUCQUOY Lines — Also attd ... assumed command of the R.A.Bde. On 17/2 remainder of G.S. Rivergal[?] ... should send to ARRAS so ... ... went to HEBUTERNE to ... 2 Scouts available. No ... ... ... F.S. APLIN-YOSTHEE, personally proceeded on 19th inst. & had his front mortars in action one hour X/19 and one for setting ... | |
| | 24-2-17 to 28-2-17 | | Month so far[?] continued. On 24/2 X/3 SNELL had an F.Bde and ... shells. On 24/6 2x/3 CARR helped X/3. Zero observed on ... been shoot through the Emplacement Church, ... | GenB[?]MDy.S |

Army Form C. 2118.

# WAR DIARY
## or INTELLIGENCE SUMMARY.

3rd Div. T.M's.  
March 1st to 31st March 1917.

(Erase heading not required.)

Instructions regarding War Diaries and Intelligence Summaries are contained in F.S. Regs., Part II. and the Staff Manual respectively. Title pages will be prepared in manuscript.

| Place | Date | Hour | Summary of Events and Information | Remarks and references to Appendices |
|---|---|---|---|---|
| ARRAS | 1.3.17 to 6.3.17 | | 9.2 mortars in action. Medium Batteries carrying out relief. Work on gun positions. Bomb stores and dug-outs etc. under R.E. Schneiders | |
| | 7.3.17 to 18.3.17 | | Work continued in construction of emplacements etc. Heavy cutting of counter battery work was carried out. Good results obtained. Lt. E.D.B. Bruce R.F.A. joined from 3rd Bn. A.S. Batt guns in trenches & killed. Several hundred of 2"&9.45" rounds of ammunition carried up to trenches. | |
| | 19.3.17 to 31.3.17 | | V/3 2nd Battery had a premature which completely destroyed the gun, emplacement, stores & ammunition, killing 1 O.R. & wounding another. Lt. T.A. HAY R.F.A. joined from 30th H.C. The howitzer object has been to cut wire. This has been steadily progressed with. Approximately 248 rounds have been fired during the month with a small percentage of blinds. A great hindrance is experienced in the gun being constantly out of action owing to Rifle mechanisms blowing back. This is due to mechanisms & O Rounds Christies Cox b/3083 m | |

**WAR DIARY**
or
**INTELLIGENCE SUMMARY.**
(Erase heading not required.)

Army Form C. 2118.

1-30 April 1917

| Place | Date | Hour | Summary of Events and Information | Remarks and references to Appendices |
|---|---|---|---|---|
| Arras | | | Medium Batteries with 5" mortar, a Stokes mortar in action provided north of [illegible] some cutting that of the heavy demolition + counter battery firing. On morning of the firing day of Infantry momentary commenced this was developed by the usual attacks at 6.30am and very precise signals, among the feats following 55 to 60 rounds fired. The work seen at out [illegible] really good, by the 6" RN observation observed [illegible] remaining by [illegible] 5/13 [illegible] I had testing the [illegible] was continuous up to and when answer was delivered to what calibre being carried. [illegible] [illegible] seen were found to be entirely satisfactory [illegible] of [illegible] [illegible] of ammunition expended from 10 am to 8 pm – 3030 rounds. No more fired from 11 pm to 8 the following morning. Work on ARTILLERY TRACKS, reaching roads, Working Parties furnished, conducting dumps of ammunition, general fatigues, away of General Infantry Equipment [illegible] to Regimental General Fatigues in billets. Buries to Arc. | |

Signed [signature]
for [signature]

# WAR DIARY
## INTELLIGENCE SUMMARY

Army Form C. 2118.

3rd D.n Trench Mortars.

Vol 7

May 1917

| Place | Date | Hour | Summary of Events and Information | Remarks and references to Appendices |
|---|---|---|---|---|
| Arras | 1st | | 3rd Div T.M. Batts have not been in action during the month. Have rendered fatigue parties as follows:— | |
| | 2nd | | Constructing dug-outs for Infantry | |
| | 3rd | | Removing from ARRAS to ACHICOURT. | |
| | 4th | | Parade & inspection — Rifle, revolver & Kit | |
| | 5th | | Constructing Shelter for 3rd Bde R.F.A. H.Q. | |
| | 6th & 8th | | Fatigue party supplied to Divnl. Parks | |
| | 9th & 10th | | " " " R.A.H.Q. | |
| | 11th-23rd | | " " " A.D.O.S. | |
| | 24th-28th | | Fatigue parties supplied to R.F.A. for work on positions & Shelters etc. | |
| | | | Remainder fatigues in Camp. | |
| | | | Working parties for Ammunition Dumps at ARRAS. | |
| | 29th | | Work in Camp — cleaning of equipment, arms etc. | |
| | 30th | | Assisted 12th Division Racing Mortars in action. | |
| | 31st | | Inspection of, & drill with, Gas Respirators. Inspection of from Ration. | |

Arnold Colston
Captain
3rd D.T.M.

A5834  Wt.W4973/M687  730,000  8/16  D.D.&L.Ltd.  Forms/C.2118/13.

To
76th Infantry Bde

## 76th T.M.B.
War diary for May 1917

| | |
|---|---|
| 1st | Returned to tunnel G.35.h from BROWN LINE |
| 2nd | Moved E of BOIS. DES. BOEUFS |
| 3rd | In reserve at HANGEST TRENCH. H.31.h. |
| 10th | Moved to BROWN LINE |
| 14th | Relieved in trenches by 87th T.M.B and marched back during the night to DUISANS. |
| 15th | At DUISANS. |
| 17th | Moved to HABARCQ. |
| 18th | Marched to AMBRINES |
| 18th to 31st | In training at AMBRINES |

3/6/17

Hu. Jeunies Smith Capt
OC 76th T.M.B

# WAR DIARY
## or
## INTELLIGENCE SUMMARY
(Erase heading not required.)

Army Form C. 2118.

| Place | Date | Hour | Summary of Events and Information | Remarks and references to Appendices |
|---|---|---|---|---|
| | 19th | | Working parties supplied to assist in construction of gunpits, dugouts etc. | |
| | | | Regimental Physical training, Rifle drill etc. daily. | |
| | 20th | | Party detailed to escort 167th Infantry Brigade to Railway, received shells. Remainder — Inspections, kit, equipment, Gas helmets & Iron Rations. | |
| | | | Night push-on 1.9.15 & 2 gunners in the line from 2/London & 13 Bn & a section of 1/3 Bn proceeded out the line to SIMONCOURT. | |
| | | | On 23rd hand over wagon lines to SIMONCOURT to the move from ORMES Parties supplied daily at SIMONCOURT to clean up roads. Remainder launching drill & general training parades. | |

Brig. Commanding
2/2 London Bde R.F.A.

3rd Div T.Ms

Army Form C. 2118.

# WAR DIARY
## or
## INTELLIGENCE SUMMARY.

(Erase heading not required.)

1st – 31st JULY -17

Instructions regarding War Diaries and Intelligence Summaries are contained in F.S. Regs., Part II. and the Staff Manual respectively. Title pages will be prepared in manuscript.

| Place | Date | Hour | Summary of Events and Information | Remarks and references to Appendices |
|---|---|---|---|---|
| SIMENCOURT | 1/7 | | 3rd Aust. Indeans moved by motor lorry to BAPAUNE. | |
| BAPAUNE | 2nd-9th | | erecting Burners, cleaning guns & equipment after usage at VIMY. 2nd Lieut T M PoR. 2/Lt J S GIBB, 10th RSF ad 2/3 Corps medically boarded to England. 2nd Lieut J A Strength on 9-7-17. Lt 3.9. APR 1/N. Q.L. MC admitted to Rest Coy Camp. | |
| BEAUMETZ-LEZ-CAMBRAI | 10th | | Induction of medium mortars full marching order. moved to BEAUMETZ-LEZ-CAMBRAI. Took over from the 1st Australian Aust. Trench mortars & 3" in the line of 2.9m5" mortars. | |
| | | | 1/3 R.M.s proceeded to the line fully equipped by 2300 hrs from Depot. Rosa Green front from Bihucourt southward. | |
| | 11/7 | | working on existing gun positions and at Rosa tramway constructing shelters. Sidings etc. | |
| | 12/7 | | Lieut C99 KIRWIN RFC and 2/Lt J H RANDALL proceeded to England. returned to coast with Lieut Postand to see a Corps dentist. 2/Lt JH RANDALL to R Army Base depot to await X-RAY fine on attachment from strap work, nothing. | |
| | 13th | | arrangement made. | |
| | 14th | | Court continued at Lieut Postand, Nesbitt, Bird & Cook commenced work. Progressed with at Rosa Postand Tank demonstration near Lieut. Proceeded here to AP. of SaH 50 prisoners in WD. | |
| | | | 132 rounds 3mch were expended during the month on obstacles | |

E.M.RANG

# WAR DIARY or INTELLIGENCE SUMMARY

Army Form C. 2118

3rd Division T.M.s
From 1st to 31st August 1917

Vol 10

| Place | Date | Hour | Summary of Events and Information | Remarks and references to Appendices |
|---|---|---|---|---|
| BEAUMETZ-lès-CAMBRAI | 1917 | | | |
| | 1st | | V/3 TMB working on gun positions. Cleaning and oiling 2-9.45" Mortars in the line. Z/3 TMB proceeded into the line to relieve V/3 TMB. | |
| | | | Remaining dugouts and deepening trenches on gun positions. Retaining Z/3 and V/3 TMB. General fatigues and gun cleaning. | |
| | 2nd | | Lieut J.A. Cousins joined on attachment from 3rd Div. Base. Work on gun positions. Fatigues joined in camp. | |
| | 3rd | | | |
| | 4th | | Marched over to 9th Divnl. Trench Mortars. 2-9.45" mortars and 3-2" mortars in the line. Accessory ammunition brought to take up their | |
| | 5th | | positions and bring out our own. No. 1 & 2 guns to awaits fixed. Went improving Gun Pit and mortaring day onto Blanes & fatigues in camp. Continued improving position. Cleaning Guns Rifles and Kilter inspection. 2 OR attached to 40th Brigade H.Q. for trailing horse drawings. | |
| | 6th | | Continued improving positions. Lewis & fatigues in camp. | |
| | 8th | | General 2" 3" shells on horse between No.1 Gun and Infantry HQ Hostile Machine Gun fire at V/2 Bn. | |
| | 9th | | Capt 2/B Bacchour rejoined from leave. | 1/24 A 50.50 |
| | 10th | | Continued work on positions V/3 TMB commenced building new position. | |
| | 11th | | Continued fatigues in camp. 13 OR attached to 40th Bde H.Q. for building drawings. | |
| | 12th | | Lieut M. Davies to Rest Camp & Mykloope & Orgeouse a temporoure admitted to Hospital. | |
| | 13th | | W.O.II.C. continued on positions. | |
| | 14th | | 2nd Lieut Grey N.D. Wickle joined on attachment from 3rd Div. Base 15.8.17 | |
| | 15th | | Lieut J.A. Stay proceeded on leave 16.8.17. | |
| | 20th | | Work on positions continued Lieut J.A. Cousins rejoined from hospital. | |
| | 21st | | Constructing dug out on bunker work as machines received 1-9.45" M.k III | |
| | 22nd | | 2nd Lieut Montan 11 OR rejoined from temp attached to H.Q. of Bde. J.S. | |
| | 25th | | Continued work on positions. Lieut Milliaro D'Estaries joined in new billets | |
| | 28th | | Lieut A.S. Wickes proceeded to 2nd Army. T.M. Depot for course of instruction | |
| | 29th | | Lieut M.B. Davies rejoined from 2nd Army T.M. Depot was effect from 2.8.17 | |
| | 31st | | & Lowrey posted from 3rd Div unit 18/7/17 respectively |  |

6 wounds 2" were fired during the month in retaliation

# WAR DIARY
## or
## INTELLIGENCE SUMMARY

Army Form C. 2118

3rd Div Trench Mortar Battery

1st to 30th September 1917

| Place | Date | Hour | Summary of Events and Information | Remarks and references to Appendices |
|---|---|---|---|---|
| MORCHIES | 1.9.17 to 6.9.17 | | Building one 9.4·5" T.M. position and one 6" T.M. position at LAGNICOURT. Gun cleaning and general fatigues | |
| | 7.9.17 | | Handed over to 56th Div 2 No; one 9.4·5" Mark II trench mortar. Moved to BAPAUME | |
| | 8.9.17 10.9.17 | | Gun cleaning, overhauling stores and personal equipment | |
| | 13.9.17 | | Inspection of Gas Respirators. Proceeded to Div Gas School ROCQUIGNY for testing same | |
| | 14.9.17 15.9.17 | | Entraining D.A.C. and field trench mortars to BAPAUME. Limb Runners to R.O.D. 14.9.17 | |
| | 16.9.17 | | Detrained at PROVEN. Horsed D.A.C. and field trench mortars marched to camp at WATOU | |
| | 17.9.17 18.9.17 | | Awaiting D.A.C. to make preparations and admitted to hospital 1 Officer and 9 o/r. Received from salvage yard | |
| | 19.9.17 | | Working parties returned to camp | |
| | 20.9.17 | | Awaiting D.A.C. grouping etc. Lieut N.A. Hunter evacuated | |
| | 21.9.17 22.9.17 23.9.17 | | Supplied party of 40 o/r for Ammunition Dump VLAMERTINGHE. Received D.A.C. | |
| | 24.9.17 25.9.17 | | 1 Officer & 36 o/r also to Ammunition Dump VLAMERTINGHE. Remainder in camp gun cleaning while awaiting orders | |
| | 26.9.17 27.9.17 30.9.17 | | Parties front of 1 Officer and 15 o/r to Ammunition Dump VLAMERTINGHE Parties proceeded from Ammunition Dump to assist pull Battery at camp. Gun cleaning etc. | |

T.B. Allen Lt R.F.A

3rd Division French Mortar
Batteries
1-31st October 1917

# WAR DIARY
## or
## INTELLIGENCE SUMMARY.
(Erase heading not required.)

Army Form C. 2118.

Instructions regarding War Diaries and Intelligence Summaries are contained in F. S. Regs., Part II. and the Staff Manual respectively. Title pages will be prepared in manuscript.

| Place | Date | Hour | Summary of Events and Information | Remarks and references to Appendices |
|---|---|---|---|---|
| WATOU | 1-10-17 to 13-10-17 | | Officers and O Ranks of personnel attached to 3rd D.A.C. and Field Batteries cleaning at ammunition dumps of the Division, and digging and making gun pits and recess for ammunition, dugouts for officers and O Ranks and helping with ammunition at the guns on the YPRES sector. 3 O.R. killed and 9 O.R. wounded. | |
| ETAPLES | 14-10-17 | | Entrained at POPERINGHE and proceeded to and spent night at rest camp at ETAPLES | |
| BAPAUME | 15-10-17 | | Entrained at ETAPLES and proceeded to BAPAUME | |
| " " | 16-10-17 17-10-17 | | Batteries employed cleaning guns and stores. 25 of personnel of medium proceeded to VAULX-VRAUCOURT, taking over some billets, and 3.2 inch guns on the BULLECOURT sector, from the 62nd D in T.M. | |
| VAULX-VRAUCOURT | 19-10-17 | | Remainder of personnel proceed to VAULX-VRAUCOURT, completed taking over billets also 6.2 inch guns in action in the RIENCOURT sector and 2-9.45 inch | |
| | 20-10-17 to 31-10-17 | | Batteries employed on wire cutting and firing in retaliation, at M8, M12, H13, J1, and M1 cutting wire in front of BOVIS trench on U21d and U22c and on the R#ENCOURT sector. Working on existing emplacements, digging and constructing positions for 6 inch Stokes and getting the guns in action | |

36 of the personnel of the 62nd and 20 of the D.A.C. were attached to assist in the construction of emplacements
2 O.Rs killed and 1 O.R. wounded of the 62nd Div during this Operations

The following amount of ammunition was expended during the period, on wire cutting and retaliation 9.45 MK I 188rds, 9.45 MK II 185 rds, 2 inch 1025, and 6 inch 114 rounds.

Christoff
Ind. O. 9.M.O. 3rd D Mortars

Army Form C. 2118

2nd Div. L.H. Batteries
From 1st to 30th November 1917

# WAR DIARY
## INTELLIGENCE SUMMARY
(Erase heading not required.)

Vol 13

| Place | Date | Hour | Summary of Events and Information | Remarks and references to Appendices |
|---|---|---|---|---|
| VAULX-VRAUCOURT | 1st to 19th | | Two medium batteries were specially engaged on the BULLECOURT sector, in digging and making gun emplacements for 6 inch Mortars, putting 6 of the guns in position and cutting wire in preparation for the assault of the infantry on the 20th inst. One medium battery and one heavy battery engaged on the RIENCOURT sector in ordinary retaliatory firing, wire cutting, and arranging special targets, and in improving present position and making additional new dug outs. | |
| | 20th | | All batteries engaged in firing on special targets as per programme of operations with the artillery. | |
| | 19th K 24th | | Batteries engaged in retaliatory firing, wirecutting etc., and improving gun emplacements, in both sectors. | |
| | 28th K 30th | | Two medium and heavy battery engaged in digging and building new emplacements for burial and of 9.45 inch mortars. Building the walls with chalk stones in the RIENCOURT sector. 8 Mortars killed (2 guns) and 8 (Number unknown) guns wounded during operations. | |
| | | | The following amount of ammunition was expended during wire cutting and retaliation purposes. 9.45 Mrtz: 105 ws guns in muzzle 182 ms, 2 inch 114 guns, and 6 inch 3146 ms. | |

E. Mash
Captain
O. I no. O 2nd Div

# WAR DIARY

**2nd Div: T.M. Batteries**

**December 1914** Army Form C. 2118.

## INTELLIGENCE SUMMARY.
(Erase heading not required.)

| Place | Date | Hour | Summary of Events and Information | Remarks and references to Appendices |
|---|---|---|---|---|
| VAULX–VRAUCOURT | 1st to 11th | | Batteries employed in the BULLECOURT sector in retaliatory firing, and answering S.O.S calls, and repairing existing emplacements in the NORREUIL sector. Pretty 6 inch and 9.45 inch T.Ms, dug-outs built, and alterations carried out in existing emplacements, also answering S.O.S calls, when asked for, and retaliatory firing. Enemy attacked in the early morning, and in the NORVUIL sector, 1 6 inch gun, and 3 2 inch were lost and the 2 inch destroyed by hostile fire. 16 O.Rs also missing. | |
| | 12th | | | |
| | 13th | | Enemy again attacked, but all remaining guns were kept in action in both sectors and satisfactorily answered all S.O.S calls. | |
| | 14th 15 19th 20th | | Batteries in NORREUIL sector engaged building new emplacements and dugouts, and putting 6 inch T.M. in position. | |
| | 21st | | Vicinity of billets heavily shelled by enemy in VAULX, two huts being destroyed, and other badly damaged. Northern Sector (Vraucourt) and 1 O.R killed and 1 Officer + 2 O.R wounded, through this shelling. | |
| | 22nd | | Rest billets shifted to sunken road, east of VRAUCOURT. | |
| | 26th to 31st | | Batteries in both sectors engaged in repairing existing positions, sapping for, and building new positions and dugouts, and attending by fr: S.O.S calls. | |
| MORY | 29th | | Rest billets moved from VRAUCOURT to south-east side of MORY. Casualties during month 1 Officer (Lieut. W.D Snedden) 1 O.R killed, 3 O.Rs wounded 16 O.Rs missing. Total ammunition expended. 9.45" shoot 22 rounds, 6 inch 328 rounds and 2 inch 129 rounds. | |

31/12/14

General, Captain
O.C T.M.O 2nd Div

www.ingramcontent.com/pod-product-compliance
Lightning Source LLC
Chambersburg PA
CBHW080846230426
43662CB00013B/2031